The ESS  of

COMPUTER
SCIENCE II

Randall Raus, M.S.
Computer Engineer and
Computer Science Consultant
Seal Beach, CA

This book covers the usual course outline of Computer
Science II. It is a continuation of *"THE ESSENTIALS
OF COMPUTER SCIENCE I"* which covers earlier,
related topics.

Research and Education Association
61 Ethel Road West
Piscataway, New Jersey 08854

THE ESSENTIALS®
OF COMPUTER SCIENCE II

Printed in the United States of America

Library of Congress Catalog Card Number 98-65422

International Standard Book Number 0-87891-671-7

WHAT "THE ESSENTIALS" WILL DO FOR YOU

This book is a review and study guide. It is comprehensive and it is concise.

It helps in preparing for exams, in doing homework, and remains a handy reference source at all times.

It condenses the vast amount of detail characteristic of the subject matter and summarizes the **essentials** of the field.

It will thus save hours of study and preparation time.

The book provides quick access to the important principles, concepts, theories and practices in the field.

Materials needed for exams can be reviewed in summary form – eliminating the need to read and re-read many pages of textbook and class notes. The summaries will even tend to bring detail to mind that had been previously read or noted.

This "ESSENTIALS" book has been prepared by an expert in the field, and has been carefully reviewed to assure accuracy and maximum usefulness.

Dr. Max Fogiel
Program Director

CONTENTS

This book covers the usual course outline of Computer Science II. It is a continuation of "*THE ESSENTIALS OF COMPUTER SCIENCE I,*" which covers earlier, related topics.

Chapter 1
ORGANIZATION OF A COMPUTER

Chapter 2
MEMORY AND INPUT/OUTPUT

Chapter 3
CODING

Chapter 4
DATA STRUCTURES

Chapter 5
PROGRAM DEVELOPMENT

Chapter 6
COMPUTER LANGUAGES

CHAPTER 1

Organization of a Computer

A computer manipulates data according to predefined rules or instructions stored in memory. Memory is organized into words containing n bits of information. The central processing unit (CPU) reads or writes one word at a time by addressing memory, then, when the memory is ready, either by reading that word or by writing new contents into that word. To perform this function, registers such as the memory address register (MAR) and the memory buffer register (MBR) are used.

Without some means of communication with the outside world, programs or data cannot be stored in memory. Therefore, input/output (I/O) devices are required. Figure 1.1 shows the basic organization of a computer. In the next three sections we will discuss in greater detail how the CPU, memory, and I/O actually work.

1.1   Central Processing Unit

Sometimes the central processing unit is presented as consisting of two parts: the control unit and the arithmetic logic unit (ALU). However, we will present the CPU as consisting of five main parts: instruction handling area, timing and control, address handling area, general purpose registers, and the ALU as shown in Figure 1.2.

1

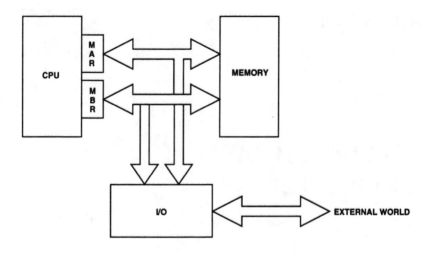

Figure 1.1 Organization of a Computer

The address handling area consists of registers in which the addresses of program instructions or required data are stored. The addresses are transferred to the MAR at the appropriate time and the read or write is facilitated by the MAR.

The ALU is constructed from combinational devices such as parallel-adders and logic gates so that arithmetic and logic operations can be performed on the data in the CPU's registers.

The instruction handling area consists of registers that contain the instruction currently being executed and the data needed to facilitate the execution of the current instruction.

The timing and control part, usually known as the control unit, sends out the appropriate clock-pulse to synchronize all components of the computer. The control unit also controls transfer of data between registers by control lines that go to the select lines of the bus system's multiplexers and decoders. This unit also controls the operation of the ALU with control lines that are connected to the ALU function inputs.

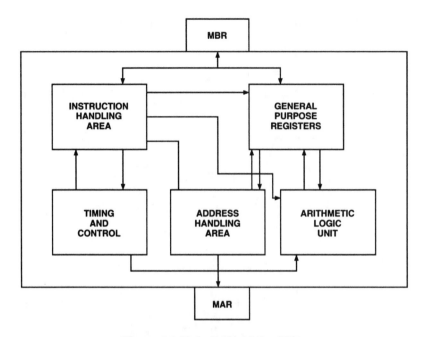

Figure 1.2 Main Parts of the CPU

The general purpose registers contain data such as the results of ALU operations or data that is temporarily being stored by the CPU so that it can be used later.

1.1.1 The Arithmetic Logic Unit

Our arithmetic logic unit has five function inputs: addition, logical complement of data A, logical complement of data B, logical AND, and logical XOR as shown in Figure 1.3. Our ALU has one additional control unit input: carry-in C, which we define as arithmetically adding 1 to the result of any operation.

Figure 1.3 also shows general purpose registers A and B, the part of the bus line that transfers data between registers A and B and the ALU, and shift register SR, which receives the output of the ALU.

3

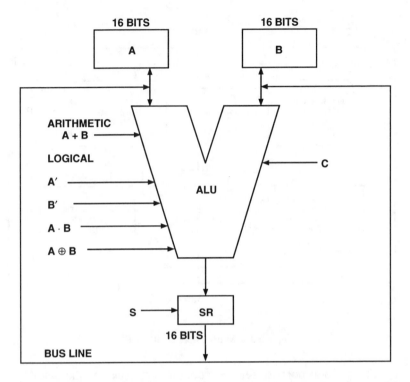

Figure 1.3 ALU, Shift Register, and General Purpose Registers A and B

The example below shows how the ALU in Figure 1.3 can be used to perform three additional operations that are not part of its function inputs.

EXAMPLE

Using the ALU in Figure 1.3, perform the following operations:

(a) A – B (subtraction)

(b) A + B (logical OR)

(c) Test if A = B

a. First enable the B' and C input functions to form the two's complement. Next transfer the contents of SR back to B. Then add registers A and B.

4

b. First complement register A, transferring the results back to A. Then do the same to register B so they now both contain their complement. Now perform a logical AND on A and B (AND every bit in register A with the corresponding bit in register B). Next, transfer the result back to A and complement A. The SR register will now contain the logical OR of A and B by DeMorgan's Law:

$$A + B = (A' \cdot B')'$$

c. Perform an XOR on A and B. The SR register will contain a zero if A = B.

The function inputs to the ALU and the select inputs to the bus system—which enable operations like those shown in the above example—come from the timing and control part of the CPU. Also coming from the timing and control part is the clock pulse. The clock pulse synchronizes the ALU operations and the bus transfers to and from registers. Each ALU operation takes one clock cycle, and each register transfer takes one clock cycle. These are called micro-operations, which will be explained more fully in Section 1.3.

1.2   Registers

Data stored in words in memory is usually relatively slow to access, about 3 or 4 clock cycles, so computers require high-speed registers that can be written to or read from in one clock cycle. These registers are "on-board" or part of the CPU.

We will give brief explanations of the different types of registers, then show how they work, in the following sections. There are nine types of registers in the computer:

1. Program Counter (PC): This register holds the address of the next instruction to be executed. It will increment on the next clock-pulse when a function input is high—this function input comes from the control unit of the CPU. Since program instructions are stored in memory in sequential order, the PC is usually incremented once per instruction. The PC is part of the address handling area of the CPU in Figure 1.2.

5

2. Instruction Register (IR): This register holds the binary code of the instruction to be executed. The instruction register (IR) is part of the instruction handling area in Figure 1.2.

3. Memory Address Register (MAR): This register holds the address of the data to be accessed in RAM. Since memory is usually much slower than CPU registers, the MAR is considered neither part of the CPU nor the RAM, but sort of a go-between. The CPU can store an address in the MAR in one clock-pulse and the MAR can hold the address lines to the RAM for 3 or 4 clock-pulses until memory is accessed.

4. Memory Buffer Register (MBR): This register is used to transfer data to and from memory. Like the MAR, the MBR is neither part of the CPU nor the memory unit, but acts as a buffer between them. It can wait 3 or 4 clock-pulses for data to be accessed in the RAM, and transfer it to or from the CPU in one clock cycle.

5. Accumulator: This register holds temporary data during calculations. The SR register in Figure 1.3 is an example of an accumulator. We will consider the SR register to be in the ALU part of the CPU.

6. General Purpose Registers: These registers generally serve as temporary storage for data and addresses. In some computers, the user may specify them as accumulators or program counters. The A and B registers in Figure 1.3 are examples of general purpose registers.

7. Index Registers: This register holds an address so that the CPU can access data anywhere in memory. Index registers incorporate the feature of a counter in that they may be automatically incremented and are usually used to sequentially access and process blocks of data. Index registers may contain a relative address and may be added to a base register or a general purpose register to obtain the actual address. Index registers are part of the address handling area of the CPU.

8. Condition Code Register (CCR): This register holds 1-bit flags which represent the state of conditions inside the CPU. Because the state of these flags is the basis for computer

decision making for conditional instructions, the CCR is part of the instruction handling area of the CPU.

9. Stack Pointer (SP): This register contains the address of the top of the stack. The SP is incremented each time the CPU stores a word of data in RAM at the address "pointed" to by the SP. The stack pointer is decremented each time the CPU uses the SP to retrieve a word of data from the top of the stack. In this way the SP allows the CPU to build up and build down a stack of data in the RAM. The SP is part of the address handling area of the CPU.

Probably the most complicated of the nine types of registers discussed above is the condition code register. We will elaborate more on the CCR now and then later show how the other registers work in Section 1.3 and Section 2.2.

There are seven basic types of flags found in most CCRs. The word "operation" in the following description refers mostly to ALU operations, but also may refer to a CPU operation that doesn't use the ALU, such as a transfer of a negative number to or from RAM.

1. Carry: This flag is set to 1 if the last operation resulted in a carry from the most significant bit.

2. Zero: This flag is set to 1 if the last operation resulted in a zero.

3. Overflow: This flag is set to 1 if the last operation resulted in a two's complement overflow, a carry into and out of the sign bit.

4. Sign: This flag is set to 1 if the most significant bit of the result of the last operation was a 1, designated a negative two's complement number.

5. Parity: This flag is set to 1 if the result of the last operation contained an even number of 1s (called even parity).

6. Half-Carry: This flag is set to 1 if the last operation generated a carry from the lower half word to the upper half word.

7. Interrupt Enable: This flag is set to 1 if an interrupt is allowed, 0 if not. An interrupt is when the program the computer is

7

running is temporarily interrupted so that the CPU may handle some other talk such as input/output from a disk drive.

Now that we have defined the different types of registers that are used to construct a CPU and have developed the concept of an ALU in the previous section, we are able to fill in more detail about the CPU that was shown in Figure 1.2. Figure 1.4 shows a CPU with eight on-board registers, an arithmetic logic unit, and two registers used to transfer data to and from RAM—the MAR and MBR. The index register X, the stack pointer, and the program counter are part of the address handling area of the CPU. The IR and CCR are in the instruction handling area, and the A and B registers make up the general purpose register area.

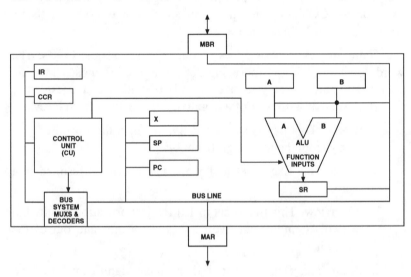

1. IR—Instruction Register-10 bits
2. CCR—Condition Code Register-7 bits
3. X—Index Register-16 bits
4. SP—Stack Pointer-16 bits
5. PC—Program Counter-16 bits
6. A—General Purpose Register-16 bits
7. B—General Purpose Register-16 bits
8. SR—Shift Register (Accumulator)-16 bits
9. MBR—Memory Buffer Register-16 bits
10. MAR—Memory Address Register-16 bits

ALU Functions
1. Addition
2. AND
3. Complement
4. X-OR
5. Carry In

Figure 1.4 Central Processing Unit – Wordlength 16 bits

8

As can be seen, the control unit can transfer data between any two registers or to the ALU's A and B inputs by controlling the inputs to the bus system's MUXs and decoders. Although not shown, there are function inputs to the X, SP, and PC, which are counter registers, to allow the CU to increment them in a way similar to a binary counter. The CU would also be able to decrement the stack pointer and shift the SR register as shown in Figure 1.5.

A close examination of Figure 1.4 makes it apparent that the index register X can be added to either the A or B general purpose registers and then the result transferred from the SR register to the MAR, making relative addressing possible. With the use of a shift register, even multiplication and division offer interesting possibilities.

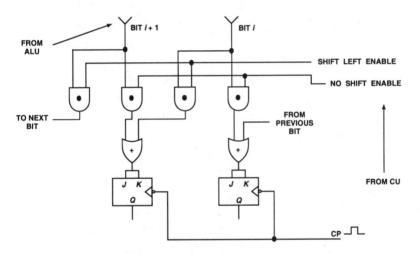

Figure 1.5 ith and ith + 1 bits of Shift Register

1.3   The Control Unit

The Control Unit (CU) is responsible for the timing and control of the central processing unit and for synchronizing the CPU with RAM. The events that take place inside a CPU are called micro-operations and what coordinates these micro-operations is the control unit.

The CU controls the CPU's micro-operations by means of con-

9

trol functions: outputs from the CU that go to inputs of the various devices that are part of the CPU. The input to the ALU that will cause it to add is a control function. The inputs to the CPU's bus system that will cause it to transfer the contents of the PC, and will cause the address of the next instruction in RAM to be executed, to the MAR is a control function. The input to a counter register, like an index register, that will cause it to increment on some clock cycles but not on others, is also a control function.

Early computers used combinational logic and synchronous design techniques, as described in Chapter 4, in order to get the CU to send the appropriate binary signals to the CPU's devices. We will show in the upcoming example the design of a simple control unit that uses combinational logic and then later by extension, the techniques used by more modern computers, but first we need to develop some basic concepts.

Register transfer language is a way of symbolically showing what micro-operations are taking place in a computer. In the following, to the left of the colon is a Boolean expression that must be logic 1 for the register transfer to take place and to the right of the colon is the register transfer:

$$XY': \text{BUS} \leftarrow A$$

The X and Y are inputs to the MUX of a bus system and the A is a register that is transferred onto a bus line. We could also write:

$$XY': \text{BUS} \leftarrow A, Z'W': \text{R0} \leftarrow \text{BUS}$$

The Z and W are inputs to the decoder of a bus system which, if held to logic 0, causes register R0 to receive the contents of the bus line. Showing both micro-operations on the same line indicates they took place simultaneously and probably on the same clock cycle because the high-speed registers of a CPU allow most micro-operations to be accomplished in one clock cycle. However, here is a micro-operation that would take more than one clock cycle:

$$\text{MBR} \leftarrow \text{M[MAR]}$$

The M represents memory or RAM, the brackets around MAR

indicate that it is the contents of the word in memory that are addressed by the memory address register and that are being transferred to the MBR or memory buffer register.

This micro-operation wouldn't take place in 1 clock cycle because RAM is slower than CPU registers, so it would probably take about 3 or 4 clock cycles for this data transfer. Because the MBR can receive data from CPU registers in 1 clock cycle and also from RAM in 3 or 4 clock cycles, it acts as a buffer between the CPU and memory. It is the control unit's job to ensure that the MAR, the MBR, RAM, and the high-speed registers of the CPU are all synchronized; more specifically, it is part of the timing function of the control unit.

The next concept we need to develop before showing the design of a simple control unit is the concept of machine language. Programs are stored in RAM in the form of 1s and 0s that can be interpreted by the CPU as instructions. A typical machine language instruction would be contained in one word in RAM. The word at the next highest memory address would also contain a machine language instruction, and so on, representing a sequence of instructions. We call this sequence of instructions a program.

The machine language instructions are transferred to the CPU, "loaded" one at a time, decoded, and executed. Actually, humans almost never write programs in machine language, but they do sometimes write programs in assembly language, which is very close to machine language. Figure 1.6(b) shows the assembly language equivalents of machine language opcodes (operation codes). Figure 1.6(a) shows the instruction format for memory reference instructions, with the opcode contained in bits 1–3. For example, if bits 1–3 of the instruction (the opcode) were 000, then the assembly language equivalent would be LDA, which would tell the CPU to load the A register from the address specified in memory by the address bits, 4–15.

11

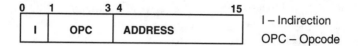

0	1	3 4	15
I	OPC	ADDRESS	

I – Indirection
OPC – Opcode

(a) Memory Reference Instruction Format

Opcode		Instruction	Comment
000	–	LDA	Load A register from memory
001	–	LDB	Load B register from memory
010	–	STA	Store A register in memory
011	–	STB	Store B register in memory
100	–	ADDA	Add A register to memory
101	–	SUBA	Subtract A register from memory
110	–	LDX	Load X register from memory

(b) Opcodes

Figure 1.6 Memory Reference Instructions

The first bit of the memory reference instruction format, shown in Figure 1.6(a), bit 0, is the indirection bit. If the indirect bit is 0, then the memory reference instruction is performed on the contents of the address in memory contained in bits 4–15 of the instruction word. For example, if the indirection bit were 0 and the opcode indicated an LDA and the address contained in bits 4–15 were binary 000000000111 or decimal 7, then the A register would be loaded with the contents of word 7 in memory. However, if the indirect bit were 1, then word 7 in memory would contain not the contents to be loaded by the A register, but the address of the word to be loaded by A. This is indirect addressing.

There is one more concept we need to develop before showing how control units work and that is register reference instructions. Figure 1.7 shows the register reference instruction formats and opcodes.

0 1 2 3 4			6 7	9 10	12 13	15

0	1 1 1	OPC	R 1	R 2	X X X

OPC – Opcode
R1 – Register 1 ID
R2 – Register 2 ID
X – Don't Care

(a) Register Reference Instruction Format

R1 or R2	Instruction	Comment
000	A	General Purpose Register A
001	B	General Purpose Register B
010	X	Index Register
011	SP	Stack Pointer
100	CCR	Condition Code Register
101	SR	Shift Register

(b) Register ID

Opcode		Instruction	Comment
000	–	Mov	Move R1 to R2
001	–	Inc	Increment
010	–	Dec	Decrement
011	–	Add	Add R1 to R2[1]
100	–	Sub	Subtract R1 from R2[1]
101	–	Xor	Exclusive OR
110	–	Cmp	Complement
111	–	Shift	Shift left

[1]Result in SR

(c) Opcodes

Figure 1.7 Register Reference Instructions

The first four bits of an instruction must be 0111 for it to be a register reference instruction format as shown in Figure 1.7(a). Bits 4–6 contain the opcodes as shown in Figure 1.7(c) and the IDs of the registers referenced are shown in Figure 1.7(b). Bits 13–15 are don't cares.

For example, if an instruction word in memory contains 0111000000001XXX, when the CPU loaded and executed that instruction it would transfer or "move" the contents of register A to register B. Another example would be if an instruction word in memory contained 0111001010XXXXXX, when the CPU loaded and executed that instruction, it would increment the index register X. The way these instructions would actually be written out by a programmer would be:

> Mov A, B
> Inc X

But the CPU would not "see" the above instructions, which are assembly language instructions. The CPU only "understands" the machine language version of assembly language consists of 0s and 1s. The assembly language program, written by a human, is converted to machine language by another program called an assembler, which stores the machine language version on disk. Later, the operating system loads the machine language program from disk into memory and causes the CPU to execute it.

EXAMPLE

A computer has the following instruction format for memory reference instructions:

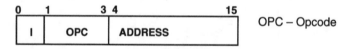

OPC – Opcode

Figure 1.8

The computer operates in four different cycles:

> Fetch Cycle (read instructions)
> Indirect Cycle (read address of operand)
> Execute Cycle (read operand)
> Interrupt

The computer has the following registers:

> PC – Program Counter
> MAR – Memory Address Register

14

MBR – Memory Buffer Register
OPR – Opcode Register
I – Indirect Register

(a) Design a block diagram for the control unit for this register.

(b) Write the micro-operations for the fetch cycle register transfer language.

The solution for (a) is — the control unit is shown in Figure 1.9.

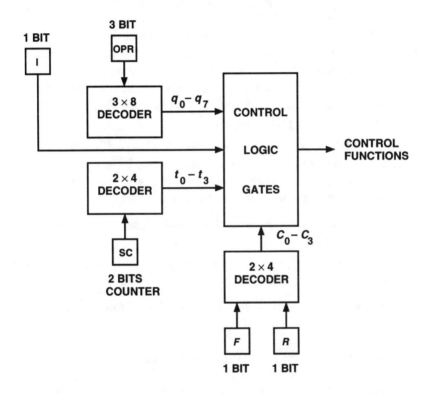

Figure 1.9

The F and R registers are used to denote which of the four cycles the computer is operating in. The 2×4 decoder associated with these registers generates four control signals, $C_0 - C_3$. Each cycle has its own control signal specified in Table 1.1.

15

Registers		Decoder Output	Computer Cycle
F	R		
0	0	C_0	Fetch Cycle
0	1	C_1	Indirect Cycle
1	0	C_2	Execute Cycle
1	1	C_3	Interrupt Cycle

Table 1.1

Each cycle is divided into four steps. Each step is designated by the output of the 2-bit binary step counter, SC. The counter starts at 00 when the computer enters a cycle, and the computer stays in the cycle until the counter reaches 11. At this point, the computer enters another cycle, and the counter returns to 00. Each step is decoded into one of four timing signals, $t_0 - t_3$.

The OPR register contains the 3-bit opcode specified in the instruction format. Each of the eight possible opcodes is decoded into eight separate control signals $q_0 - q_7$. Each signal specifies one of eight instructions from the instruction set of the computer.

The I bit is bit I of the instruction format. It is used to designate indirect addressing.

All of these signals go to the control logic section, which then carries out the actual instructions through the control functions.

The solution for (b) is — each cycle consists of four steps:

$$t_0, t_1, t_2, t_3.$$

During the fetch cycle, the instruction is read from memory. The memory location which contains the instruction is specified in the PC register. In most computers, the instructions are stored sequentially in memory. That is, the next instruction is at the location of the previous instruction plus one; hence, the PC will be incremented during each fetch cycle. The fetch cycle is designated by the C_0 control signal.

A step is specified when the control signal expression to the left of the colon is true (Logical 1).

$$C_0 t_0: \quad \text{MAR} \leftarrow \text{PC} \qquad \text{(Step 1)}$$

In the first step of the fetch cycle, the contents of the PC, which contain the location of the next instruction to be read from memory, are transferred to the MAR.

$$C_0 t_1: \quad \text{PC} \leftarrow \text{PC} + 1 \quad ; \quad \text{MBR} \leftarrow \text{M[MAR]} \qquad \text{(Step 2)}$$

Two operations take place in the second step of the fetch cycle: (1) The PC is incremented so that it will specify the location of the next instruction when the next fetch cycle occurs. (2) The contents of memory, whose address is specified by the MAR, are transferred to the MBR; hence, the MBR contains the instruction code. These two operations occur simultaneously, with both operations having equal importance.

$$C_0 t_2: \quad \text{I} \leftarrow \text{MBR}_0 \quad ; \quad \text{OPR} \leftarrow \text{MBR}_{1-3} \qquad \text{(Step 3)}$$

Again, two operations take place in the third step of the fetch cycle: (1) The contents of bit 0 of the MBR are transferred to I. This bit specifies whether or not the data in the instruction will be indirectly addressed. (2) The contents of bits 1 through 3 of the MBR are transferred to the OPR. Once the opcode is in the OPR, it will be decoded into one of eight possible signals, $q_0 - q_7$.

$$I c_0 t_3: \quad \text{R} \leftarrow 1$$

or

$$\bar{I} c_0 t_3: \quad \text{F} \leftarrow 1 \qquad \text{(Step 4)}$$

Different operations take place in the fourth step of the fetch cycle, depending on the status of the I register. If the I register is 1, then there is an indirect memory reference instruction, so one must go to the indirect cycle. The computer goes to the indirect cycle by letting the R register become 1 and leaving the F register 0. When F and R are decoded, the C_1 control line is excited, which designates the indirect cycle.

The second statement states that when there is a memory reference instruction, go to the execute cycle.

The computer goes to the execute cycle by letting the F register become 1 and leaving the R register 0. When F and R are decoded, the C_2 control line, which designates the execute cycle, is excited.

As the example above shows, a simple control unit for a CPU can be designed using combinational logic connected to the appropriate sequential logic. The whole control unit would fall under the category of synchronous sequential circuit. The combinational logic part of the CU in the example above was not shown, but obviously would be fairly complicated. But what if some instructions took more than four micro-operations to execute, and what if there were not 15 memory reference and register reference instructions as we showed in Figures 1.6 and 1.7, but 100, or 200, with some of them taking as many as 20 or 30 micro-operations to execute?

Early computers were designed using synchronous sequential circuits for control units, what is referred to as hard-wired. It soon became impractical, because of the enormous complexity of the combinational logic required to hard-wire CUs. What emerged as the answer was "firmware." Firmware is not hardware and not software, but somewhere in between. The device that makes firmware possible, the ROM for read-only memory, is shown in Figure 1.10.

A ROM cell is much simpler than a RAM cell. Figure 1.10(a) shows eight word lines, $W_0 - W_7$, with diodes connected to four bit lines, $B_0 - B_3$. If a word line is addressed and there is a diode connection between that word line and a bit line, then that bit will be logic 1, otherwise logic 0. The diode connections on the word lines not addressed have no effect, because current cannot flow backward through a diode.

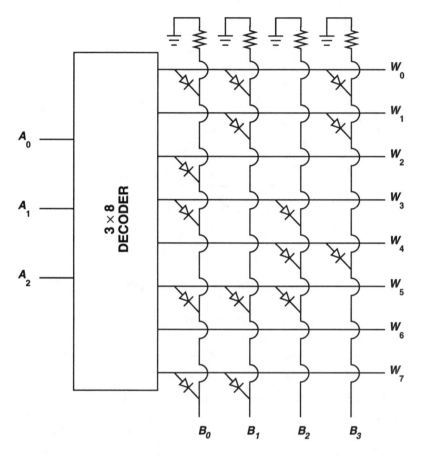

Figure 1.10(a) 8-Word By 4-Bit ROM

Getting back to the concept of firmware, the combinational logic part of the control unit in the previous example could be replaced by a ROM, and the step counter and F and R registers could be replaced by a counter register, which we will call a micro-program counter (μPC). The micro-program counter could be connected to the ROM's address lines (see Figure 1.10(b)), and the ROM's diodes could be affixed in such a way that as the μPC is incremented, the ROM will output the appropriate control functions to the CPU's devices, for each step, or micro-operation, in an instruction cycle.

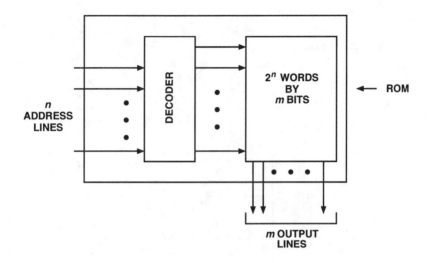

Figure 1.10 (b) Basic ROM Structure

However, for this scheme to work, the control unit must have conditional branching capability. For example, after the fetch cycle is completed, if the indirect bit of the instruction register is high, the control unit should then branch to the indirect cycle.

In addition to the control functions, the ROM must also contain the branch addresses. Thus, the data contained in the ROM, called firmware, looks more and more like a micro-program. It is this concept of two programs being executed—the program stored in RAM, and the micro-program stored in the ROM on the CPU—which executes each step, or micro-operation of the instructions of the main program—which makes modern computers work. In effect, there is a computer within a computer, the CU, which is sometimes called a micro-computer within the larger computer, which consists of the CPU, RAM, and input/output devices.

Figure 1.11 shows our new control unit.

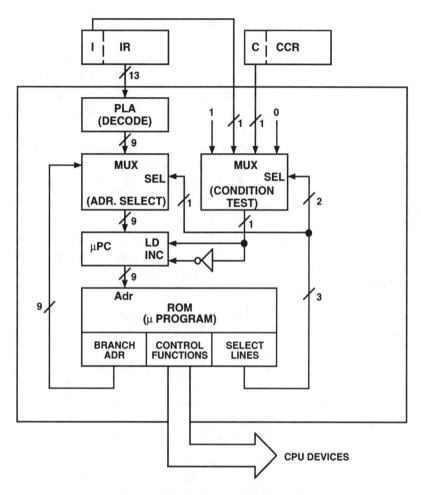

Figure 1.11 Control Unit of the CPU

Actually ROMs are usually slower to access than RAMs; however, special high-speed ROMs have been developed for firmware applications. Another CU device that requires high operational speed is the PLA, for programmed logic array, which decodes, or maps, the instruction contained in the IR to the address to be loaded into the μPC, as shown in Figure 1.11.

Sometimes complex decoders, or ROMs, are used to map the IR to the beginning address, in ROM, of the sequence of micro-operations that are stepped through for that instruction's execution cycle. But we choose the PLA because of the flexibility it allows the designer, as shown in Figure 1.12. For example, the address bits of the memory reference instructions (see Figure 1.6) are, in effect, don't care conditions as far as the control unit's PLA is concerned. Don't care conditions are handled simply by not connecting either the input or inverted input as shown in Figure 1.12(a) for input I_1 and word-line W_2, thus, if I_0 is a 1, W_2 is output regardless of I_1's value.

Once the instruction has been mapped to a ROM address by the PLA, whether that address will be output by the address selection MUX is determined by the first of three bits of the select field of the ROM's output as shown in Figure 1.11. If the first bit of the select field is a 0, the address mapped by the PLA will be selected; if that bit is a 1, the branch address output by the ROM will be selected.

Whether the address selection MUX's output will be loaded is determined by the second and third bits of the select field which are the select inputs of the condition test MUX. If those two bits form binary 0, then the input of the MUX which is held at logic 1 is selected and the output of the condition test MUX causes the μPC to load the output of the address selection MUX. If the select inputs of the condition test MUX are binary 3, then the input which is held at logic 0 is selected, and the μPC is incremented.

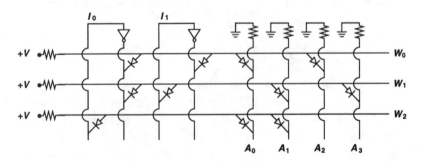

(a) PLA with 2 Inputs, 3 Product Term, and 40 Outputs

22

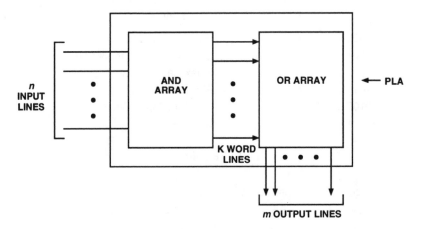

(b) Basic PLA Structure

Figure 1.12 Programmed Logic Array

However, if the select input of the condition test MUX is binary 1 or 2, then one of the two conditional inputs is selected, namely the indirect bit of the instruction register or the carry bit of the CCR. If the indirect bit is selected as the conditional input and the indirect bit is high, it could result in a branch to the indirect cycle, depending on the branch address field and the select input of the address selection MUX.

If the carry bit is selected as a conditional input, it would have a number of possible uses; however, we will have to delay describing them until the introduction of our extended instruction set shown in Figure 1.13.

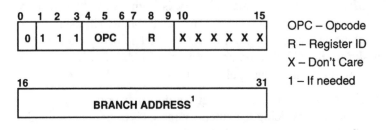

OPC – Opcode
R – Register ID
X – Don't Care
1 – If needed

(a) Instruction Format

23

R	Register	Comment
000	A	General purpose register A
001	B	General purpose register B
010	X	Index Register
011	SP	Stack Pointer
100	CCR	Condition Code Register
101	SR	Shift Register

(b) Register ID

Opcode		Instruction	Comment
000	–	BSR	Branch to subroutine
001	–	BRC	Branch if carry is high
010	–	PUSH	Push register on stack
011	–	POP	Pop register from stack
100	–	LDAR	Load A register from adr. R + X ‡
101	–	STAR	Store A register to adr. R + X ‡
110	–	RET	Return from subroutine
111	–	BRA	Branch unconditionally

‡ Address is formed by adding index register X to register specified in register ID field–bits 7–9.

(c) Opcodes

Figure 1.13 Extended Memory Reference Instructions

The only instruction in the extended instruction set that would be affected by the use of the carry bit of the CCR as a conditional input is the BRC instruction: branch if carry is high. Now, bear in mind there are two conditional branches. The macro branch, if taken, causes the machine language program in RAM, that is being executed sequentially by the CPU, to branch to another address in RAM, where the CPU will resume sequential execution.

The micro branch, if taken, causes the micro-program in high-speed ROM, that is being executed by the CU, to branch to another location in ROM where the CU will step through a sequence of micro-operations that will cause the macro branch to be executed.

24

Let us assume the last instruction before the BRC was an addition resulting in a carry; then, after the CU fetched the BRC instruction and began the execution cycle, the carry input into the condition test MUX would be high, causing the μPC to load the branch address resulting in this sequence of micro-operations.

$$PC \leftarrow PC + 1$$
$$MAR \leftarrow PC$$
$$MBR \leftarrow M[MAR]$$
$$PC \leftarrow MBR$$

The reason the PC would be incremented by 1 is because the address for the macro branch would be in the first word following the word that contained the opcode for BRC. In other words, the BRC instruction takes up two words, which is the definition of an extended instruction.

After the new address for the micro branch is transferred from the MBR to the PC, the macro branch is completed. The CU would then micro branch to the fetch cycle prior to executing the next instruction.

Another possible use of the carry bit of the CCR, as a conditional input of the control unit, could be multiplication. Our instruction set does not include a multiplication instruction, so it would have to be an assembly language subroutine. However, it would be easy to redesign our instruction set to include more instruction by increasing the opcode field.

Multiplication of binary numbers is basically shifting and adding. If we added another shift register to the CPU and gave it what is called end around carry capability, as shown in Figure 1.14, the multiplier could be held in the new shift register.

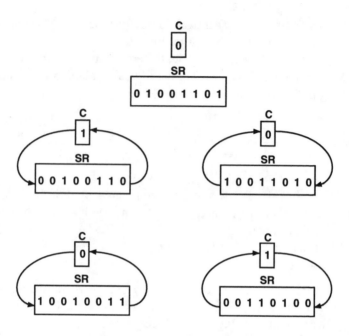

Figure 1.14 8-Bit Shift Register with End Around Carry

Figure 1.14 shows an 8-bit shift register for space saving purposes, but our CPU has 16-bit registers.

Once the CPU has two shift registers, one could be used to shift the multiplicand. The other one could be used to shift the multiplier through the carry with the carry bit used as a condition test by the control unit so that the micro program would branch to micro-operations that either shifted and added the multiplicand to the accumulated result, or just shifted it.

One of the advantages of using an end around carry for multiplication is that the multiplier is fully restored upon completion of the operation, so it can be used for another instruction.

Computer multiplication is actually more complicated than what we have described. There are overflow conditions and other factors to contend with. Division, although basically shifting and subtraction, is more complicated still. Other factors adding to the complexity of computer arithmetic are various types of fixed point and floating point operations and efforts to at least make partial products and partial quotients the result of parallel operations. However, in the final analysis, all computer multiplication and division boils down to shifting and adding and shifting and subtracting.

The machine language of a computer, and by extension its assembly language, is designed in tandem with the computer's architecture, and especially the architecture of the control unit. In the next section, we will see how the design of the memory unit, input/output, and interrupt handling interplay with the computer's machine language.

CHAPTER 2

Memory and Input/Output

One of the definitions we gave for computer architecture was that part of the hardware the programmer was interested in, especially the system's programmer. This section should make it clear why that is a good definition.

2.1 Memory

The program counter on the CPU we have been describing contains 16 bits, which means it is capable of addressing 2^{16} or 65,536 (usually described as 64K) words in memory. The address portion of the memory reference instructions we showed in Figure 1.6 of the previous chapter contained 12 bits, so a memory reference instruction would be capable of addressing anywhere in the first 2^{12} or 4096 words of memory. If the indirect bit of a memory reference instruction was a 1, then a memory reference instruction could address anywhere in the 64K of memory, but the memory location that contained the indirect address would have to be somewhere in the first 4096 words of memory.

Figure 2.1 shows the memory space addressable by the CPU in Figure 1.4 and how it might be mapped.

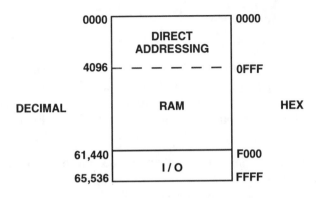

Figure 2.1 Memory Space Map

The first F000 hex of the addressable memory space shown in Figure 2.1 could be RAM with the first 0FFF hex capable of direct addressing. The memory space from F000 hex to FFFF hex, or the last 0FFF hex would be allocated for input/output. We will explain more about I/O in Section 2.2.

In a multiprogramming system, memory must be allocated by the operating system for more than one user program. Figure 2.2 shows the most straightforward approach to this problem which is to simply allocate memory to each program in ascending address spaces.

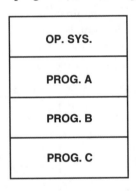

Figure 2.2 Multi-Program Memory Allocation

There are two immediate problems with the previous scheme. The first is the operating system problem might use all of the direct addressing space. One way of solving this problem is to add a segment register to the CPU that would contain the beginning address of the currently running program. This would allow each program to have its own low memory and direct address space. Another solution is to redesign the instruction set and the CPU so that all addressing is relative.

Even if the direct addressing problem has been resolved, there is the question of how to keep programs from interfering with each other. One way is to add two registers to the CPU which hold the lower and upper address boundaries of the program that is currently running. The operating system could load those registers with the boundaries for each program before it dispatched the program—and then grant the program a time slice and start to run it. The CPU would also have to be redesigned, either by altering the micro program or by some kind of hard wiring, so that any write or branch outside of a program's assigned area would result in an unmaskable interrupt—one that is not affected by the interrupt bit of the CCR. It would then be up to the operating system to terminate the program.

All of the above changes amount to a great deal of complexity. Maybe there is a simpler way. Perhaps the 64K of memory could be considered a page and each program could use its own page. Figure 2.3 shows a paged memory allocation scheme, with sixteen 64K pages for a total of one mega-word. Since one mega-word requires 20 address lines, a page could be addressed by the upper four lines.

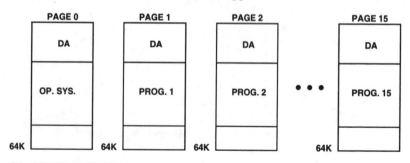

DA – DIRECT ADDRESSING

Figure 2.3 Paged Memory Allocation

30

A page register could be added to the CPU to hold the upper four address lines, while the MAR could operate as it normally does. If the application program was unaware of the page register, it could operate as it normally does. If the program was too large for 64K of RAM, it could be divided into segments and swapped back and forth from disk. If the system was multi-user as well as multi-programming, the user would get the impression of virtual memory larger than 64K.

This approach also leads to complications. Instructions would have to be added to allow the application programs to perform I/O through the operating system (see Figure 2.3) because page 0 would be the only page with I/O access. This would mean redesigning the CPU. Also, it should be noted that disk swapping creates a very complex technical problem, for both the system programmer and the computer architect.

Another problem with the paged memory allocation we have described is a loss of flexibility. If each program is allotted a fixed amount of memory, even though some may need half that much, then memory is wasted that could go to another program that is forced into a slower disk swapping mode. In other words, we have traded flexibility for simplicity.

Any design process includes weighing tradeoffs and making decisions. The main point is that making a computer a multi-programming system requires changes in the computer's architecture.

2.2 Input/Output

Any computer must have some way of communicating with the external world. It does this by means of interfaces with input/output devices such as keyboards, monitors, printers, disk drives, modems, etc.

There are basically two types of I/O: programmed I/O and memory mapped I/O.

Programmed I/O requires a separate I/O channel on the CPU as shown in Figure 2.4. This channel is similar to the channel which accesses the memory unit and includes a buffer register and an address register or may be constructed with a bus line that multiplexes the I/O devices with some of the CPU's register.

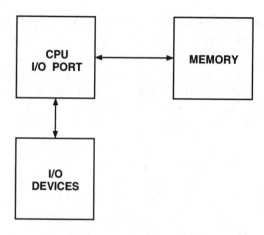

Figure 2.4 Programmed I/O

Programmed I/O also requires separate instructions to be added to the computer's instruction set. Here is a possible example:

Stdout B

This assembly language instruction might cause an alphanumeric character to be output through the I/O channel to the standard output device which might be defined as a monitor. Of course, micro-code would have to be added to the firmware to allow the CPU to handle this and any other input/output instructions.

The second basic type of I/O is memory mapped I/O, which allocates a portion of the memory address space as shown in Figure 2.1. This has the advantage of not requiring a separate I/O port on the CPU. Also, no additional instructions need to be added because memory reference instructions can perform I/O.

The chief disadvantage is that application programs can access peripheral devices directly, bypassing the operating system which normally arbitrates conflicting I/O requests to prevent system lockup. This can be prevented by only allowing programs to access their own space, as described in Section 2.1.

Once the decision has been made to use programmed I/O or memory mapped I/O, there is still the question of how the CPU is to know when an I/O device is ready for a data transfer. Simple computers use a technique called polling. Once the CPU gives a peripheral device a command, it keeps checking the device's status, or polls, until the device is ready for a data transfer. Because I/O devices are much slower than computers, a lot of time can be wasted polling and waiting.

Most computers, including an increasing amount of personal computers, use a technique called interrupt driven I/O. The I/O device is given a command, then the status of the program requesting I/O is changed to blocked, and another program is allowed to run, or is dispatched. When the I/O device is ready for a data transfer, it signals the CPU by means of an interrupt. The program that is running is interrupted, the operating system handles the data transfer, and changes the status of the program requesting I/O to ready, so it will run on its next time slice, then returns control of the CPU to the interrupted program.

Both programmed I/O and memory mapped I/O can be interrupt driven.

Figure 2.5 shows how the interrupt control lines are connected to the control unit of the CPU.

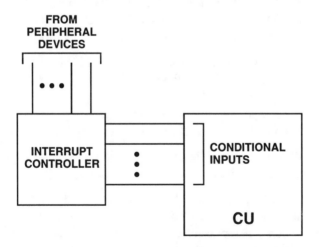

Figure 2.5 Interrupt Control Lines

Our computer will use memory mapped, interrupt driven I/O. The best way to show how this would work is by showing an example that is part of an operating system program. Figure 2.6 shows the first part of this program, which is the data part in direct addressed or low memory.

Adr.	Contents			
		ORG 0H		
0000	9000	DSK–VEC	WORD	9000H
0001	A000	PRT_VEC	WORD	A000H
0002	B000	KBD_VEC	WORD	B000H
		ORG 100H		
0100	0000	ZERO	WORD	0000H
0101	F001	DSK_BUFF	WORD	F001H
0102	EF00	RAM_BUFF	WORD	EF00H
0103	FF00	DSK_CNT	WORD	FF00H

Figure 2.6 Interrupt Handling Data

The three columns on the right are written by a programmer; the first two are added in front by the assembler. The first field is the address in RAM, and the second field shows the contents of that memory location after the program is loaded into memory.

As we said, the third, fourth, and fifth fields are written by the programmer. The third field is the label field, which is referred to by later program statements. The fields marked WORD tell the assembler to put the following hex value in that memory location. Notice the second and fifth fields are the same for every word statement.

The ORG is an assembler directive which tells the assembler the beginning address of the next series of statements.

In Figure 2.6 the address 0000 contains the addresses to the disk interrupt handler. This is called a vector. The next two words in memory, which are represented by the next two lines, contain the printer interrupt vector and the keyboard interrupt vector.

34

If we added a small ROM to the CPU, connected it to the bus line, and stored the values 0000 hex, 0001 hex, and 0002 hex, in binary, in the ROM, the CPU would have access to the address of these vectors.

If the interrupt control lines were added as conditional inputs of the control unit, as shown in Figure 2.5 and the interrupt bit of the CCR was also added as a conditional input, then the firmware could be modified to check, following every execution cycle, if interrupts were enabled, and if so which, if any, required servicing.

If the disk interrupt, for example, was high, the CU could push the contents of the program counter onto the stack, so it could be recovered when the interrupted program resumed execution, move the address of the disk vector (0000 hex) to the MAR, load the disk vector (9000 hex) from address 0000 hex, and transfer it to the PC. Then the CU could branch to the fetch cycle, and the CPU could resume execution just like any other program.

Figure 2.7 (below) shows that part of the operating system which handles the disk interrupt.

Adr.	Contents			
		ORG 9000H		
9000	F500	DSK_INT	PUSH	CCR
9001	F400		PUSH	A
9002	F440		PUSH	B
9003	F480		PUSH	X
9004	0100		LDA	ZERO
9005	8100		MOVE	CCR,A
9006	6101		LDX	DSK_BUFF
9007	9102		LDB	RAM_BUFF
9008	F9C0	DSK_LOOP	LDAR	,X
9009	FA40		STAR	B,X
900A	7280		INC	X
900B	7240		INC	B
900C	0103		LDA	DSK_CNT
900D	7200		INC	A
900E	F200		BRC	END_DSK

Adr.	Contents			
	9013			
9010	2103		STA	DSK_CNT
9011	FE00		BRA	DSK_LOOP
9013	F000	END_DSK	BSR	SCHEDULER
	C000			
9015	F680		POP	X
9016	F640		POP	B
9017	F600		POP	A
9018	F700		POP	CCR
9019	FC00		RET	

Figure 2.7 Disk Interrupt Handler

Notice the line in Figure 2.7 with address 9004; the contents are 0100 hex. Compare this with the address of ZERO in Figure 2.6.

The reason they match is because the machine language instructions, which are what the second field represents, are put together as they were described in Figures 1.6, 1.7, and 1.13.

The disk handler pushes registers CCR, A, B, and X onto the stack so they can later be restored for the program that was interrupted, as shown in Figure 2.8—the CU automatically increments the stack pointer each time. Then the disk handler proceeds to move 0 into the CCR to disable interrupts, until the disk I/O is completed.

Next, the disk interrupt handler loads the index register X, the memory address allocated to the disk drive's data buffer. It then loads the B register with the offset to the buffer in RAM that the data is transferred to.

The program then loops through the DSK_LOOP, using relative addressing to transfer 256 words or data from the disk to the RAM. When the DSK_CNT reaches its limit, a carry is generated causing a branch to END_DSK.

Next, the disk handler branches to the SCHEDULER subroutine so the status of the program which requested the I/O can be changed to ready from blocked.

Finally, all registers are restored from the stack and the return statement causes the PC of the program that was interrupted to also be restored from the stack, so it can resume execution.

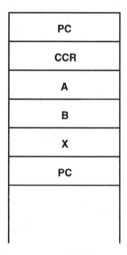

Figure 2.8 State of Stack During Disk I/O

Figure 2.8 shows the state of the stack just after the subroutine call to the SCHEDULER was made. The first PC on the stack would be 9015 hex, the return address from the SCHEDULER. The second PC would be the address of the program that was running when the interrupt occurred.

The stack is addressed by the SP, the stack pointer, which is incremented each time there is a PUSH, an interrupt, or a subroutine branch, BSR. The SP is decremented each time there is a POP or a return, RET.

CHAPTER 3

Coding

Digital computers not only process numbers, but also handle characters like letters of the alphabet and certain special characters. There is also the problem of transmission errors that can crop up when data is transmitted from peripheral devices such as disk drives, keyboards, and modems. Even internal transfers using computer bus systems can sometimes result in erroneous data. In this chapter, we will discuss codes that have been developed to facilitate data handling and error detection.

3.1   Common Character Codes

Most handling of alphanumeric characters is done using the American National Standard Code for Information Interchange (ASCII). There have been competing standards for coding alphanumeric characters such as EBCDIC, or Extended Binary Coded Decimal Interchange Code, which is similar to ASCII. However, EBCDIC has increasingly fallen into disuse.

ASCII uses 7 bits to represent 128 characters, including the upper- and lowercase letters of the alphabet, the ten decimal digits, punctuation marks, and certain special non-printable characters. The eighth, or most significant bit of each byte, is called the "parity bit" and is used for error detection, which we will discuss in the next section.

Table 3.1 shows the ASCII character set. For the sake of brevity, Table 3.1 represents the hex equivalents, but ASCII characters are, of course, transmitted and stored in binary by digital computer systems.

| | | Bits 4 to 6 | | | | | | |
| | | First Hex Digit (MSB) | | | | | | |
Bits 0 to 3 Second Hex Digit (LSB)	0	1	2	3	4	5	6	7
0	NUL	DLE	SP	0	@	P		p
1	SCH	DC1	!	1	A	Q	a	q
2	STX	DC2	"	2	B	R	b	r
3	ETX	DC3	#	3	C	S	c	s
4	EOT	DC4	S	4	D	T	d	t
5	ENQ	NAK	%	5	E	U	e	u
6	ACK	SYN	&	6	F	V	f	v
7	BEL	ETB	'	7	G	W	g	w
8	BS	CAN	(	8	H	X	h	x
9	HT	EM	)	9	I	Y	i	y
A	LF	SUB	*	:	J	Z	j	z
B	VT	ESC	+	;	K	[	k	{
C	FF	FS	,	<	L	/			/
D	CR	GS	~	=	M	]	m	}
E	SO	RS	.	>	N	^	n	≈
F	SI	US	/	?	O	_	o	DEL

Table 3.1 ASCII Character Set

When a key on a computer keyboard is depressed, it is usually the binary representation of the ASCII character that is transmitted to the computer; when alphanumeric characters are stored in RAM or on disk drives, it is usually in their ASCII representation.

The characters LF and CR from Table 3.1, when transmitted from a computer to a printer or monitor, will cause these devices to either perform a line feed or a carriage return. The character FF from Table 3.1 will cause a printer to perform a form feed.

When a user types on a keyboard, the ASCII character is received by the computer, interpreted by the program currently running on the computer, and then transmitted to the monitor, although this happens so fast it appears to the user that there is a direct connection between the monitor and the keyboard. Thus, there is sometimes no response when a key is depressed, because the program currently running may be doing other things, such as sorting a disk file or displaying graphics data on the monitor. In some multi-user systems, there are simple terminals which insure that the ASCII characters are displayed on the monitor when a key is depressed even if the computer itself doesn't respond immediately.

Another common use of the ASCII standard is the transmission of data over telephone lines and cables. The unprintable character ACK shown in Table 3.1 stands for "acknowledge" and is used to communicate to the computer that sent the message that the message was received. NAK, from Table 3.1, stands for "not acknowledge," and usually results in a retransmission. STX, which stands for "start of text," is another example of a non-printable character used for remote transmission.

One of the advantages of ASCII representation is that it can easily convert decimal digits to BCD (binary coded decimal) representation simply by clearing bits 5 and 6. Humans usually work with numbers in decimal form. Computers usually convert decimal numbers to binary, perform calculations or manipulations, then convert them back to decimal. BCD, which uses four binary digits to represent the equivalent of 0–9 using binary 0000 through 1001, can avoid the conversion process. Some computers have special BCD adders and subtractors to perform arithmetic operations on BCD numbers. Calculators which only have decimal keypads and function keys usually use some kind of BCD representation.

3.2 Error Detection

3.2.1 Parity Checking

As mentioned in the previous section, ASCII representation is often used for transmission over phone lines or cables, with the parity bit or check bit placed in the most significant bit position. If "odd" parity checking is used, the parity bit is set to a 1 if bits 0–6 contain an even number of 1s, so that the total number of high bits is odd. If "even" parity checking is used, the parity bit is set to 1 if bits 0–6 contain an odd number of 1s.

Because telephone lines and cables usually only allow transmission over a single line, the ASCII characters must be transmitted in serial form, as shown in Figure 3.1.

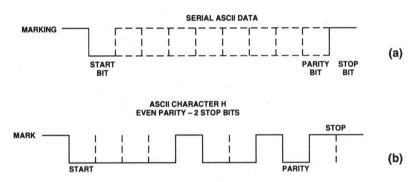

Figure 3.1 Serial Data Transmission

Serial data transmission usually starts the transmission by lowering the voltage on the transmitter for a specified time period, the start bit in Figure 3.1, then transmits the character bits including the parity bit, and then raises the signal voltage for one or two bits, the stop bit(s) shown in Figure 3.1(a) and Figure 3.1(b). After that, the transmitter can either transmit the next character, by lowering the signal, the start bit again, or idle by keeping the signal high.

This is called "asynchronous" data transmission because there is no clock-pulse synchronizing the sending and receiving devices as described in the section covering sequential circuit design.

Errors are detected by the receiving device keeping track of the number of 1s, including the parity bit. If odd parity is used, the number of 1s should be odd, or there is at least one invalid bit. Even parity checking works the same way in reverse. Parity checking is an effective error checking method when the error rate is low enough that there is almost never more than one incorrect bit in each byte. In fact, some computers use parity checking for RAM, adding an additional parity bit for each word.

41

The "baud rate" is the number of symbols transmitted per second. In the case of binary signals, each bit is a symbol, so a transmission rate of 9600 baud, using the character bit timing described in Figure 3.1(a), would transmit 960 characters per second.

3.2.2 Hamming Code

Parity checking is an effective way of detecting errors when the error rate is low, but suppose we want to not only detect errors but also correct errors.

Imagine we want to design a code with m message bits and r check bits that will allow all single errors to be corrected. There is such a code, which was achieved by using a method developed by Hamming (1950). The bits of the code word are numbered consecutively starting at the left, with the bits whose numbers are powers of 2 being check bits, and the rest data bits. Each check bit forces the parity of itself and some collection of bits to be even or odd.

To find the check bits to which the data bit in position K contributes, K is rewritten as a sum of powers of 2. For example, $11 = 1 + 2 + 8$. A bit is checked by just those check bits in its expansion. An example of how a Hamming code works is shown in the example below.

EXAMPLE

Assume messages of length $m = 7$ are being transmitted using a Hamming code. Show how to check for an error and, if necessary, correct it for the following codeword:

1100111

We will initialize a counter to 0, then as the message arrives, we will examine each check bit, and if it is invalid, add it to the counter. If the counter is 0, the message will be accepted as valid.

Since the bits whose position are powers of 2 are check bits, we know that bits 1, 2, and 4 are check bits.

check bits

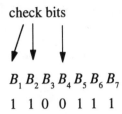

$B_1 \ B_2 \ B_3 \ B_4 \ B_5 \ B_6 \ B_7$

1 1 0 0 1 1 1

Since any bit that is not a check bit is a data bit–B_3, B_5, B_6, and B_7 are data bits. To see which check bits a data bit in position K contributes to, rewrite K as powers of two:

(1) $3 = 1 + 2$, so B_3 is checked by B_1 and B_2
        $5 = 1 + 4$, so B_5 is checked by B_1 and B_4
        $6 = 2 + 4$, so B_6 is checked by B_2 and B_4
        $7 = 1 + 2 + 4$, so B_7 is checked by B_1, B_2, and B_4

In the Hamming system each check bit forces a collection of bits including itself to even or odd parity. We know from (1) above that B_1 checks

$$B_3 = 0$$
$$B_5 = 1$$
$$B_7 = 1$$

so B_1 should be 0 for even parity, but

$$B_1 = 1$$

so B_1 is invalid and we add 1 to the counter.

Similarly, B_2 checks

$$B_3 = 0$$
$$B_6 = 1$$
$$B_7 = 1$$

so B_2 should equal 0, but $B_2 = 1$, so we add 2 to the counter.

And similarly B_4 checks

$$B_5 = 1$$
$$B_6 = 1$$
$$B_7 = 1$$

so B_4 should equal 1, for even parity, but $B_4 = 0$, so we add 4 to the counter.

The counter is now 7, so B_7 is the incorrect bit. We change $B_7 = 1$ to $B_7 = 0$, and the correct message is:

1 1 0 0 1 1 0

CHAPTER 4

Data Structures

Data structures are collections of data that are related. Vectors and matrices are examples of data structures. A library card catalog is a more complex data structure, with cross referencing between data items.

There are many kinds of data structures, but for computer programming purposes, they can nearly all be manipulated by casting them into one of the data structures we will describe in this chapter.

When a programmer creates an algorithm to solve a problem, he also creates a data structure that is manipulated by the algorithm. The processing speed and amount of storage can be greatly affected by the choice of data structure. If n is some natural parameter of a problem, the computation time may be proportional to 2^n for one data structure and proportional to n for another.

4.1 Arrays

The one-dimensional array is the simplest data structure. An array is a list of items such that each item may be uniquely identified by its index. The individual data items are called the array's elements or components. The type of the array's components is all the same and is referred to as the base type or component type. An array may be an array of integers or an array of reals.

The array is the best known data structure and is widely used in almost all computer languages. Arrays may be of multiple dimensions, but we will confine our discussion of arrays in this chapter primarily to arrays of one dimension. The following is a Pascal language declaration of an array.

Var
    Example_Array : array [1..10] of integer;

Most languages require that the array be declared in some way—then, when the program is loaded and run, sufficient space in memory is set aside for the array. The disadvantage of this is that during actual execution the program may not require as much memory as anticipated, or may require more. This results in either wasted memory or in a run-time error. To compensate for this, recent versions of some languages are allowing dynamic array declarations during run time.

The problem of memory allocation, though, is really minor compared with the inefficient algorithms programmers are tempted by because of the deceptive simplicity of the array structure. The following Pascal statement allows us to traverse (examine each element of) an array A:

for $i := 1$ until N do
    examine $(A[i])$;

The above statement represents what is called a "linear search algorithm." If there were 100 elements in the array A, it would take 100 searches for the procedure "examine" to find the data item it was looking for. To generalize, to perform a sequential search of a list of N data items that is represented by a linear array requires a time proportional to N.

Next we will consider the problem of sorting an array of numbers. One possible algorithm is the "bubble sort," which is essentially a "quick-and-dirty" method. The bubble sort algorithm can be described as follows:

1. Set a flag to 0.

2. Scan the data array from one end to another.

3. Examine pairs of numbers on adjacent words, and if the number with the higher index is numerically smaller, exchange the numbers, and set the flag to 1.

4. When the scan is completed, if the flag is not 0, return to step 1, otherwise exit.

The name "bubble sort" refers to the tendency of small numbers in the above algorithm to "float" to the top of an array. The bubble sort is simple to implement in almost any language, which accounts for its popularity. But again, it is the deceptive simplicity of the array structure which leads programmers into implementing inefficient algorithms.

In the next section, we will show much more efficient algorithms for sorting and searching arrays.

4.2 Tree-Structured Data Structures and Algorithms

The importance of trees in data structures cannot be attributed to any one, or even a few, applications. LISP (List Processing Language), which is the language used most often in artificial intelligence research, uses trees as its primary data structure. Although artificial intelligence and LISP, at least so far, have not emerged as major players in the computer industry, trees have many other applications.

4.2.1 Rooted Trees

A rooted tree is a graph which consists of nodes and branches, with each branch connecting two nodes. As shown in Figure 4.1, the node at the upper end of a branch is called the predecessor node, and the node at the lower end is the successor node.

In order for a tree to be a rooted tree, the following properties must be satisfied.

1. There is a unique node (*R* in Figure 4.1), which has no predecessors. This is called the root node.

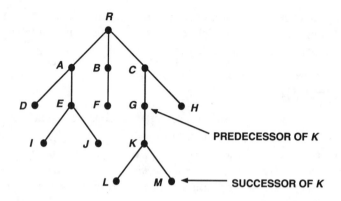

Figure 4.1 Rooted Tree

2. Every node other than the root node has precisely one predecessor.

3. Every node other than the root is connected to the root by a
unique path. That path begins at the root and ends at the
node. Every node on the path, except for the root, is a successor to the previous node.

An ordered tree is a tree in which each of the successors of a
node is ordered. In Figure 4.1, for example, D is the first successor of
A and E is the second successor.

Every node of a tree other than the root node is called a branch
node. The degree of a node is the number of successors; for example,
Node E is degree 2 and Node F is degree 0. If a node has no successors, it is called a leaf.

The concept of subtree is important in tree-structured algorithms.
Each interior node (a node with a successor) is the root of a subtree
consisting of its successors.

It would seem that it would be difficult to represent a tree structure in the memory of a computer, but we will show in the next two
sections how trees can be represented by simple data structures such
as arrays and stacks.

4.2.2 Representing Trees as Arrays

A traversal of a data structure is a scan in which each element is examined exactly once. If we are going to represent a tree as an array, we must first find a way to traverse a tree. Remember our simple algorithm for searching a one-dimensional array:

> for $i := 1$ until N do
> examine $(A[i])$;

This represents a traversal of an array.

A binary tree is a rooted tree in which every node has at most two successors. We will use this special class of trees to demonstrate traversal. Later we will show how any rooted tree can be represented by a binary tree. Figure 4.2 shows an example of a binary tree.

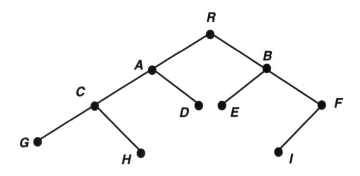

Figure 4.2 A Binary Tree

As we mentioned in the previous section, every node in a tree can be considered the root of its own subtree. Thus, subtrees can be broken into smaller and smaller components. The algorithm for a postorder traversal of a binary tree is:

Postorder Traversal

1. Traverse the left subtree in postorder

2. Visit the root

3. Traverse the right subtree in postorder

The example below shows a postorder traversal of a binary tree that is used to represent an arithmetic expression.

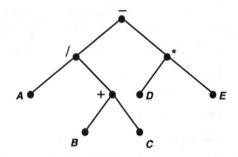

Figure 4.3 Tree Representation of A / (B + C) – D * E

EXAMPLE

Perform a postorder traversal of the tree in Figure 4.3.

Visit all the nodes of the left subtree of –, then –, then all nodes of the right subtree of –. The nodes before – have to be visited in the order that the node in the left subtree of / are visited, then /, and then the nodes of the right subtree of /.

By continuing with this reasoning, the postorder traversal of Figure 4.3 is found to be:

$$A \: / \: B + C - D * E$$

This example shows that an arithmetic expression can be represented by a binary tree, but does not resolve the ambiguity created by the missing parenthesis. We will attempt to reconcile that in the next section.

There are two other algorithms that will effectively scan a binary tree, the preorder and endorder traversals, but we will concentrate on postorder. The example above showed a recursive algorithm, an algorithm that keeps repeating itself. The algorithm descended down a branch. Until it found some kind of limit, in this case a node with no subtree, then the algorithm backed up until it found another branch it could descend down, until finally the algorithm had run its course when it had traversed the right subtree of the root.

There is a natural affinity between recursive algorithms and trees, which is why this data structure keeps reappearing. In fact we will use a recursive algorithm to represent a tree using an array, but first we give another example of a recursive algorithm shown in Figure 4.4.

Function $f(x$: Integer): Integer;
Begin
       If $x = 0$ then $f(x)$: $= 1$;
       else
       $f(x)$: $= x * f(x - 1)$;
End; (* End Function f *)

Figure 4.4 Recursive Algorithm to Compute Factorial

You will notice that the algorithm shown in Figure 4.4 to compute the factorial of an integer keeps making recursive calls on itself until it reaches some kind of limit, in this case when f: $= 1$, then starts returning almost like it's traversing back up a branch of a tree.

Figure 4.5 shows a Pascal procedure that will perform a traversal of a binary tree structure stored in an array, although in this case it is a two-dimensional array, so we can identify the left and right subtrees.

Procedure Postorder (n : Integer);
Comment – A is a two-dimensional array with A [n, 1] identifying the left subtree and A [n, 2] identifying the right subtree. Integer n is initialized to 1 by the calling procedure.
Begin
       if A [n, 1] $< > 0$ then Postorder (A [n, 1]);
       examine (A [n, 0]); (* Data in $A[n, 0]$ *)
       if A [n, 2] $< > 0$ then Postorder (A [n, 2]);
End; (* Postorder *)

Figure 4.5 Procedure to Traverse a Binary Tree in an Array

Even though the above recursive procedure is only three lines, it would obviously take more CPU time to traverse a tree structure than to simply perform a linear search of an array. However, suppose the data items of a binary tree were ordered, then it would be a snap to find the data item we were searching for. Figure 4.6 shows the comparison that might be made when searching for a data item stored in an ordered binary tree.

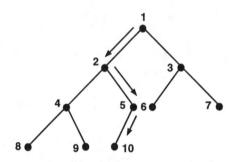

Figure 4.6 Search of Ordered Binary Tree

The search of an ordered binary tree is proportional to $\log_2 n$. In other words, if there were 128 items stored in the tree, the time would be proportional to 7 because $2^7 = 128$, while a linear search of an array of 128 items would be proportional to 128.

Although we won't show it, there is an algorithm called Floyd's algorithm that will perform an elegant sort of a binary tree stored in an array. Surprisingly enough, Floyd's algorithm can be implemented in about 20 lines of code in a language that allows recursion. Also, a new data item can be added with at most $\log_2 n$ comparisons. This is far more efficient than a Bubble sort of a linear array.

It is the efficient sorting and adding and deleting of new items which is the biggest advantage of storing data in an ordered binary tree. Actually data items that are stored in a linear array in order can be searched efficiently using what is called a "binary search," which eliminates half of the array each time a comparison is made.

We have shown that a binary tree can be traversed or scanned, stored in an array, and used for efficient sorting and searching algorithms. But what we don't have is a binary tree. What we have is an ordered rooted tree, but some of the nodes have more than two branches as shown in Figure 4.7(a).

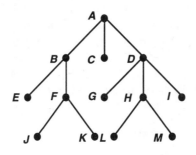

(a) Ordered Rooted Tree

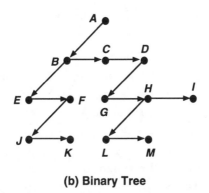

(b) Binary Tree

Figure 4.7 Conversion of an Ordered Rooted Tree to a Binary Tree

As it turns out, any ordered rooted tree can be represented as a binary tree. The following describes how to represent an ordered tree as a binary tree as shown in Figure 4.7(b):

1. There is a one-to-one correspondence between the nodes in T and T'.

2. The first successor of a node in T is the left successor of the corresponding node in T'.

53

3. The second to nth successor of a node N in T are linked in T' as a chain of right successors. The chain begins at the node in T' that corresponds to the first successor of N.

We have shown how a tree structure can be stored in an array; however, the stack can also be used to store and reconstruct a tree. Earlier in this section we attempted to represent an arithmetic expression using a tree representation, but failed to resolve ambiguities arising from operator precedence. We will attempt to resolve those ambiguities in the next section.

4.2.3 Polish Notation and the Stack

The Polish mathematician Lukasiewicz showed arithmetic operations in prefix notation, as follows:

$A * B$ Infix notation

$*AB$ Prefix notation

Postfix or reverse Polish notation, represents the operators after the operands.

$AB*$ Postfix notation

We will use reverse Polish notation or Postfix notation to evaluate a tree representation of an arithmetic expression by storing it on a stack, but first a few words about stacks.

We saw in the previous section how trees are recursive structures, that algorithms and procedures that traverse and sort trees are recursive in that they call on themselves as the traversal or sort is performed. We have also seen how a stack is used to store the return address and needed register contents prior to a subroutine call. In fact, when a recursive procedure that is sorting or traversing a tree calls upon itself, a stack is used to store or "remember" the state of the procedure, much like a stack is used for subroutine calls. All this suggests there is some kind of affinity between a tree structure and the stack. We will try to develop this concept further as we discuss representations of arithmetic expressions.

Figure 4.8(a) shows an arithmetic expression that is represented by an ordered tree, and Figure 4.8(b) shows the ordered tree converted as in Figure 4.7.

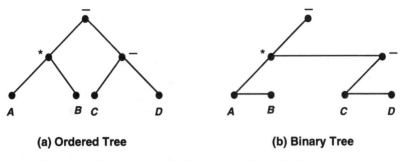

(a) Ordered Tree　　　　　　　　**(b) Binary Tree**

**Figure 4.8 Rooted Ordered Tree for Arithmetic Expressions
and its Corresponding Binary Tree**

If the binary tree in Figure 4.8(b) were traversed in postorder, the linearized representation that would result would be:

$$AB * CK \setminus -$$

which is the reverse Polish notation for the original arithmetic expression. The advantage to this representation is that it does not require parentheses to resolve inherent ambiguities regarding operator precedence. Figure 4.9 shows the states of a stack that would be used to process the above linear representation. Notice that, in effect, the original tree representation is being reconstructed, although the symbol VAL stands for value, and it is the values of the variables and results of operations that would actually be stored on the stack.

The use of the stack to evaluate arithmetic expression converted to reverse Polish notation works for any arithmetic expression, no matter how complicated, although the stack allocation would of course be much deeper than shown in Figure 4.9.

Except for a few computers with stack-oriented architectures, most computers do not use Polish notation to evaluate arithmetic expressions, but modern compilers that generate what are called *N*-tuples are similar in concept to postfix representation with the major difference being they include explicit references to results of intermediate computations. An example of *N*-tuples is shown in Figure 4.10.

55

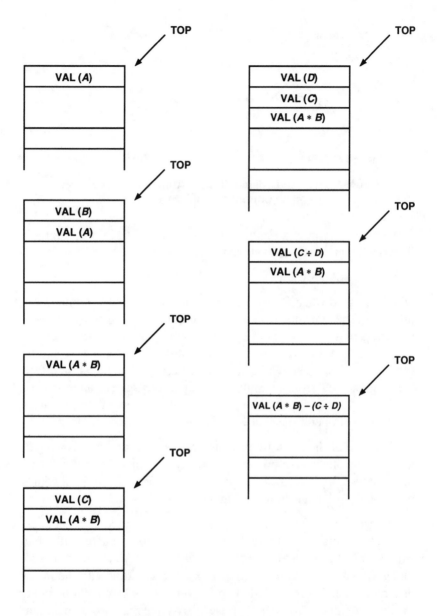

Figure 4.9 States of Stack While Processing $AB * CK \setminus -$

Now we have a way to not only efficiently evaluate arithmetic expressions, but to reconstruct linear representations of ordered rooted trees, both using the stack.

(1)   (MULT, Addr(b), Addr(c), 11)

(2)   (FLOAT, Addr(b), 12)

(3)   (MULTF, Addr(b), Addr(d), 13)

(4)   (FLOAT, 11, 14)

Figure 4.10 N-tuple Representation

Compilers call a parser subprogram, which stores a parse tree, an array. The parser in turn calls the semantic analyzer which stores information on what is called the semantic stack in the form of records. Modern compilers are always implemented in a language that allows recursion. Again, we get a tree stored in an array and the natural affinity of trees, recursive algorithms, and the stack.

4.3 Queues

A queue is a type of list structure with the limitation that items may be deleted at either end but not in the middle. The term *queue* is also used in connection with computer memory to mean a group of items chained together sequentially by address.

One type of queue is known as a FIFO queue, which stands for "first-in first-out." Items are added to the FIFO queue at one end and deleted at the other. When the term *queue* is used in computer science, the FIFO queue is usually meant.

One simple application of a queue applies to customers arriving at a ticket window. When a new customer arrives, he is placed on the queue. When a customer buys a ticket, he is deleted.

4.4 Hash Tables

We have described in previous sections a linear search of an unordered array, a binary search of an ordered array, and a tree search of an array organized into a rooted, ordered, binary tree. The binary search of an ordered array is fast and efficient, but the insertion and deletion of data is inefficient. A rooted, ordered, binary tree may be searched efficiently, and data may be inserted and deleted efficiently and quickly. However, there are times when an even faster method is required, especially with a very large number of elements to be inserted in the structure.

A hash table is a data structure that can be used for storing large amounts of data. The advantage of a hash table is that the operations of insertion, deletion, and searching are much more efficient. The tradeoff is that more memory is required.

An example of a hash table could be an array of records with each record having two fields: 1. a character string which represents a data item, and 2. an integer which contains the index of another record in the array. When the array is initialized, the array is divided into two parts: 1. the main hash table, and 2. vacant memory. If we have an array with a maximum size of 10,000, the first 5,000 records could be considered the main hash table, and the second 5,000 records could be considered vacant memory. When the hash table is initialized the integer fields of the records of the main hash table are initialized to 0. When vacant memory is initialized, the integer field of the record indexed by 5,001 is initialized to 5,002, the integer field of the record indexed by 5,002 is initialized to 5,003, and so on, up to 10,000. We say the records of vacant memory are "linked" and that the integer field "points to" the next record in vacant memory.

A data item's location in the hash table is computed by subjecting it to a hash function. A typical hash function could be: addition of the ASCII values of the individual characters (assuming the data items are character strings), division by 4, and multiplication by 3. A hash function can be anything the programmer defines it to be; however, the hash function should result in the data items being distributed as evenly as possible in the hash table.

When the first data item is stored in the hash table, it is subjected to the hash function. If the result of the hash function is, for example, 50, the data item is stored in the character field of the record indexed by 50. If the hash function result for the second data item is 34, it is stored in the record indexed by 34; however, if the result is 50, which is already taken, the data item is stored in the first location in vacant memory—the record indexed by 5,001. Then, three things happen: 1. the integer field of the record indexed by 50 is changed to 5,001, so that it points to the new data item; 2. an integer variable that keeps track of the first location in vacant memory is updated to 5,002; and 3. the integer field of the record at 5,001 is changed to 0, indicating the end of this particular "chain" of data items.

The above results in two types of "chains": 1. the chain of records in vacant memory, and 2. individual chains of data items whose hash function result is the same. This technique is called "bucket hashing."

When the hash table is searched, the data item being searched for is subjected to the hash function, then linear search is performed of the data items with the same hash function result—with the integer fields used as pointers to successive records. If the hash table is evenly distributed, only a few records need to be searched.

Deletion is left as an exercise for the reader. However, as a hint, when an item in vacant memory is deleted, the no-longer-used record should be linked to the chain of unused records.

An important application that uses hash tables is compilers. A compiler may create a huge hash table of all the identifiers of an entire program, with an additional field added to the array's records. This additional field would contain a descriptor, or a pointer to a descriptor, of each identifier and how it is used.

CHAPTER 5

Program Development

In the 1950s and '60s, programming was an art form and the tools of the programmer were flowchart templates and decks of punched cards. Since then, there has been an explosion in the capability and sophistication of computer technology and with it demands for much more sophisticated software. This has given rise to the academic and professional disciplines of computer science and software engineering in order to bring as much structure as possible to the process of developing programs.

Software development has been called the most complex endeavor by human beings. The phrase "intellectual management of complexity," attributed to structured programming pioneer Edsgar W. Dijkstra, has become synonymous with programming. Jim O. Elijogu, in his 1991 book *Software Engineering With Metrics*, interpreted an article written by Dr. Dijkstra in the early seventies as an attempt to signal to the computing industry the real nature of the monster it had engaged as if in a battle. Leo J. Levy, of Bell Laboratories, entitled his 1987 book on software engineering economics *Taming the Tiger*.

By contrast, it is often the programmer, who is a rationalist, whose goals are simplicity and elegance of design, who creates the most manageable software. The preceding paragraph should not be interpreted as an attempt to intimidate the computer science student, because some real tools have been developed to facilitate software development, or "tame the tiger." It is merely an admonition to use those tools.

5.1 Structured Programming

In structured programming, the emphasis is on a smooth flow of the program from beginning to end. To accomplish this, the programmer should use a minimum number of branches to other parts of the program.

Structured programming emphasizes standardization of program design concepts and methods. Two aspects of these are top-down design and module independence, which we will elaborate on in Sections 5.1.3 and 5.1.4.

5.1.1 Flowcharts

People tend to relate easily to pictures, which is why programmers use diagrams to communicate among themselves and with their clients. A diagram provides a clear-cut picture that allows a designer to visualize a problem or pinpoint an error.

There are numerous references in computer science literature to flowcharts being obsolete. Flowcharts are blamed for the complicated spaghetti programs of the sixties and seventies and are said to be replaced with more sophisticated diagrams such as data flow diagrams, which we will describe in Section 5.2, "Software Engineering." However, flowcharts are still in use. They are a good way to describe a basic algorithm and are still sometimes used in the detailed design phase of software engineering.

There are three fundamental logic structures used in computer programming:

1. Simple Sequencing

2. Decision Making

3. Repetition or Looping

Figure 5.1 shows how each is represented using a flowchart.

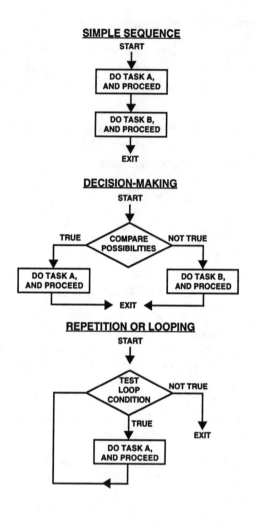

Figure 5.1

An example of a task might be an assignment statement such as $J = I * 2$ in FORTRAN. An example of decision making might be the IF-THEN-ELSE construct which is common to many languages. An example of repetition or looping is the Pascal WHILE loop.

62

5.1.2 Pseudocode

Pseudocode is a combination of a computer language and English. Computer languages that are most often used in pseudocode are the ones that are closest to English like Pascal and ADA.

In computer science literature, pseudocode has all but replaced flowcharts as a way of showing algorithms. Figure 5.2 shows two examples of algorithms taken from an operating systems text.

(a) if $s > 0$
      then $s \leftarrow s - 1$
   else BLOCK calling process on s
      DISPATCH a ready process

(b) procedure PRODUCER
     local record
     begin
       produce record
       APPEND (record, buffer)
       number $\leftarrow$ number + 1
       SIGNAL (number)
     end

Figure 5.2 Examples of Pascal Pseudocode

The above examples were selected to show how easy it is to describe an algorithm, even in a subject the reader is not familiar with, using pseudocode. When using pseudocode, assignment statements are shown symbolically using arrows such as when $s - 1$ is assigned to s in Figure 5.2(a). Processes to be performed are shown in capital letters, followed by a short description in English of what the process does. Procedure calls are also shown in capital letters with an informal description of their parameters in parentheses. Reserved words of the languages are often highlighted in bold, and variables are often italicized.

Pseudocode is ideal for a program development technique called stepwise refinement. A programmer might write down a description of a module mostly in English, then on the next step, rewrite the

63

module actually showing what statements are part of a process or actually declaring some of the variables and in this way systematically refining the program to compilable code.

5.1.3 Modular Programming

The idea of modular programming is to subdivide a problem into manageable parts, or modules. In other words, divide and conquer. One of the reasons Pascal is used so much for teaching is because it is a block-structured language that encourages modularity.

When most programmers think of modules, they think of procedures and functions or their equivalent. Technically, the definition of a software module is a group of statements that can be compiled separately.

However, it is generally good programming practice to use separate procedures and functions for program modules. Modules should be as discrete and separate as possible, with the variables worked on by the module declared locally, with only the parameters returned to the calling procedure changed. One of the most important rules of structured programming is one point of entry and one point of exit for each module. With procedures and functions used for modules, there is automatically only one point of entry. There should be only one return statement or exit point in a module.

Another important concept of modular programming is functional cohesiveness. Modules or subprograms should be functionally cohesive, with the statements and tasks limited to those that just do one thing. Figure 5.3 shows an example of a module that is not functionally cohesive.

```
Procedure CALLING
   Var
        Global_Index
        Array_Of_Int
        Length, Width, Area, Total
   CONST Max_Index = 3
        •••
        •••
Procedure FIND_AVG_AREA (Avg, Area)
   Begin
        Total ← 0
        FOR Global_Index = 1 to Max_Index by 1
             Total ← Total + Array_Of_Int [Global_Index]
        Avg ← Total / Max_Index
        Area ← Length * Width
   End
```

Figure 5.3

The procedure FIND_AVG_AREA, in the above figure finds the average of an array of these integers and the area of a rectangle. This is the opposite of functional cohesiveness, because this subprogram does two completely different things. There should be separate procedures or functions, one to find the average of the array, and one to find the area of a rectangle.

Another problem with the procedure FIND_AVG_AREA is that it changes the nonlocal variables Global_Index and Total which are declared in the calling procedure. Perhaps the calling procedure is going to use Global_Index and Total for another purpose that won't work if these values are changed. These variables should be declared locally, perhaps named Local_Index and Local_Total. It doesn't really matter what the programmer calls them, which is a question of style, but they should be declared locally and worked on locally, if at all possible.

Modules should be as separate and discrete as possible and should be functionally cohesive. Programming practices like those shown in

Figure 5.3, if used in a large program, can lead to deep logic errors that can take an enormous amount of time to debug. On the other hand, if modules have been kept separate, bugs can be isolated to subprograms. The programmer will also find that his thinking has been organized with less chance of logic errors cropping up.

5.1.4 Top-Down Programming

Top-down programming is an important concept of structured programming and utilizes both the divide and conquer approach of modular programming and the concept of step-wise refinement mentioned in the section on pseudocode. A useful tool for top-down programming is the structure chart which is shown in Figure 5.4.

Suppose a programmer wanted to design a program to process a payroll, a structure chart could be used to graphically describe what might be called a level one design as shown in Figure 5.4(a). Then, as the next step in the design process, the programmer could break the major functions into smaller more manageable subprograms or modules as shown in Figure 5.4(b).

One of the most important concepts of structure charts is that they are hierarchical or tree-like, with the main program being the root node and the modules forming the branch nodes.

Getting back to the payroll program example, the programmer would continue breaking the program into smaller modules, one level at a time, until the detailed design phase of the program was reached. Since structure charts are not suitable for detailed design, pseudocode could be used for the detailed design. Assuming the payroll program had reached the detailed design phase after only two levels (real programs are seldom this simple), a pseudocode refinement of block 3.1 of Figure 5.4 could be:

COMPUTE gross pay
    begin
        COMPUTE regular pay
        COMPUTE overtime
        COMPUTE shift differential
    end

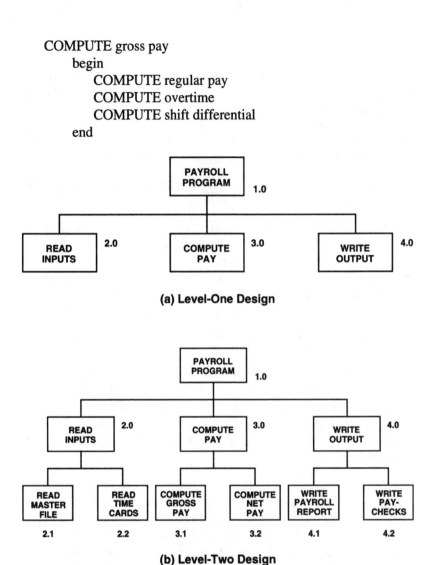

(a) Level-One Design

(b) Level-Two Design

Figure 5.4 Structure Chart

The detailed design could continue with a few more steps of refinement until the pseudocode was close to actual code, the actual coding could then be a simple transition from the detailed design to compilable code.

5.1.5 Debugging

One of the principal objectives of structured programming is to minimize the time spent debugging programs, which is often the greatest time sink in the process of software development. Programmers often spend many hours at computer terminals playing a trial-and-error game, if their program doesn't work they'll change something, and if it still doesn't work, they'll try something else, and so on.

However, there are ways to systematically and methodically avoid this time sink.

Programmers should be familiar with their code. The generous use of comments is a good way to gain familiarity with a program. Programmers often put comments in their program later, thinking that comments serve the purpose of helping someone else read or work with their code. But thoroughly commenting on a program reinforces an understanding of how it works.

Each subprogram should have a header explaining what it does and all the variables that are changed by that subprogram should be listed in the header with a brief description of what they do. Every line in a program that is not immediately clear should have a comment explaining it. At the same time, not a lot of time should be spent explaining statements that are obvious. Comments should be written cryptically and with dispatch and should read more like notes then well-crafted prose.

Another way to gain familiarity with a program is to "walk-through" the code prior to debugging. Many programmers paper compute their program by running simple numbers through it, keeping track of the values of variables for each step on graph paper. Paper computing, in addition to catching easy to find errors, results in a deep understanding of the algorithm's logic and program flow.

One of the advantages of structured programming is that the inherent modularity allows subprograms to be tested separately. In fact, every program module should be tested and debugged separately, using a dummy main program to feed it data. When all of the subprograms are working, they can be put together to test the main program.

Debugging of either the main program, or a subprogram, should be done methodically. If a program has twenty lines of code and doesn't work, a write statement of all the variables should be inserted at line ten. If, upon rerunning, the values at line ten are correct, a write statement should be inserted at line fifteen; if not, one should be inserted at line five. In a manner similar to a binary search, the bug can quickly be pinned down to its exact location.

The advantage of doing everything systematically and methodically is that it allows speed. A good programmer is very thorough but works fast. Only when a particularly complex problem crops up does he slow down for deep thought.

5.1.6 Summary of Structure Programming

Fundamental Theorem of Structured Programming: A given software problem can be refined into modules that correspond hierarchically to the nodes of a tree, with the final irreducible functions corresponding to the leaves of a tree, and with each child node having only one parent node.

Computers see programs as a sequence of instructions to be executed, but the human mind can only relate to an organized structure. There is a difference between complex and complicated. The human mind has no problem with a complex subject that is broken down into understandable parts, but draws a blank when confronted with a complicated spaghetti flowchart.

The flow of a program should be like the traversal of a rooted tree described in the chapter on data structures, except that not all the nodes are visited, depending on the input. Because the main program, or root of the tree, may be a loop, the tree may be traversed many times.

5.2 Software Engineering

Software engineering was created partially as a result of the structured program revolution of the early seventies and partially to deal with the so-called software crisis.

The software crisis, or at least the perception of a crisis, was caused by the improvement in computing power of the hardware by orders of magnitude, while the productivity of the average programmer only doubled. This resulted in a greatly increased share of cost of software in the development of a new computer system. The cost of software development and maintenance is projected by some analysts to become as high as ten percent of GDP sometime after the turn of the century.

Another reason for the perception of a software crisis was that studies showed the cost of maintenance of software during the software life cycle as anywhere from 50 percent to 80 to 90 percent of the total cost of the software, while the cost of maintaining equipment was nowhere near that. It was thought that these costs could be contained by bringing engineering discipline to software development.

Software engineering has now been around for more than 20 years, and the results have been mixed. There has not been a dramatic increase in the productivity of the programmer, but there may have been some breakthroughs in the works, such as automatic code generation.

5.2.1 Software Life Cycle

The software life cycle consists basically of 1) definition, 2) development, and 3) maintenance. These can be expanded by what is known as the waterfall model as shown in Figure 5.5.

The software requirements phase, as shown in Figure 5.5, involves the communication of three types of people.

1. The user, who is not technically trained, but has a list of user desires.

2. The analyst, who is trained in the technicalities of software production.

3. The designer, who is proficient at designing methodologies.

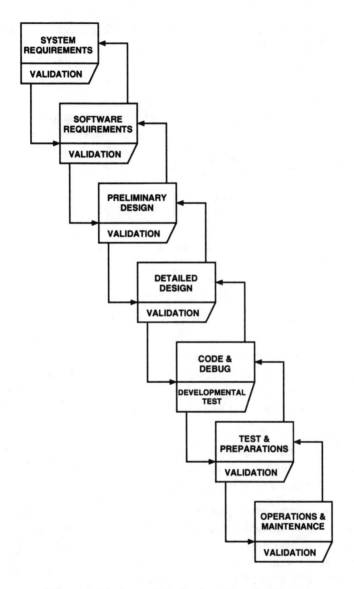

Figure 5.5 Software Life Cycle – Waterfall Model

The output of the requirement phase is the software specification which includes data flow diagrams as shown in Figure 5.6, func-

71

tional specifications, and may include HIPO charts as shown in Figure 5.7. The idea of the software specification is that good specification will allow a good design.

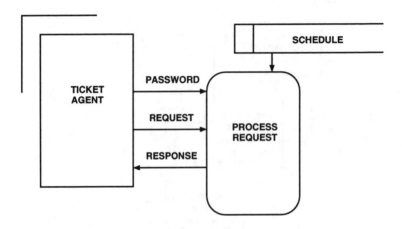

Figure 5.6 Example of a Level 1 Data Flow Diagram

The preliminary design phase utilizes structure charts to specify the system's architecture and perhaps HIPO charts. It has been estimated that perhaps 60 percent of system errors are a result of design errors, so there has been increased emphasis on getting the design right.

The detailed design phase utilizes pseudocode or perhaps flowcharts, or perhaps SPD (standard program design) notation which has become common in business applications.

Once the detailed design phase has been completed, the system's modules are coded and debugged during the development test. When all of the subsystems are working, they are put together for the preoperations validation. They are then shipped to the user and the maintenance phase of the software life cycle begins.

One of the theories behind developing a system with a high degree of modularity is that maintenance costs can be lowered by pulling out and plugging in new modules almost as if a software system were a machine, as errors are found or the original requirements prove to be inadequate.

This section has contained a brief description of the software life cycle, which is a principle of the relatively new disciplines of software engineering. We will close this section with the most widely accepted definition of software engineering, which came from Dr. Frederick L. Bauer (1972): "The establishment and use of sound engineering principles (methods) in order to obtain economical software that is reliable and works in real machines."

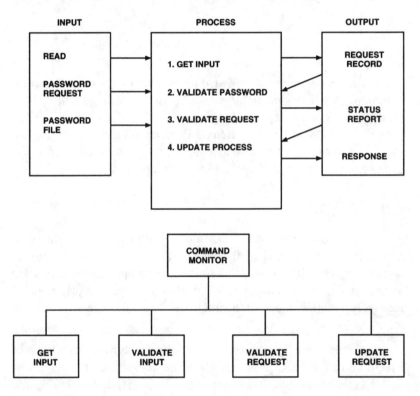

Figure 5.7 HIPO (Hierarchical Plus Input-Process-Output) Chart

CHAPTER 6

Computer Languages

In the first chapter we provided an overview of some of the most commonly used computer languages. Now we will go into a little more detail concerning the languages of BASIC, COBOL, FORTRAN, Pascal, and Object-Oriented Programming. We have chosen these five to provide a basic understanding of what is involved in the development, design, and application of computer languages.

6.1   BASIC

BASIC was developed at Dartmouth College and introduced in 1965. The primary goal of the language at that time was to make computers accessible to students so that the computers could be used as ordinary tools for academic work. It is a simple language with a relatively small number of instructions, and this makes it easy to learn.

Statements are numbered sequentially to indicate the flow of execution of a BASIC program. There are also statements that allow for changing the flow. These are GOTO, GOSUB, RETURN, and FOR-NEXT. BASIC is often implemented as an interpreted language. This allows a user to run the program without having to go through a compilation stage. An interpreted program is usually slower than one that has been compiled. BASIC is available on many large systems and almost every microcomputer.

One of the control structures available in BASIC is the FOR-NEXT loop. This is an example of a counted loop, one in which the number of times throughout the loop is specified by the values in the FOR statement. For example, the statement

$$100 \text{ FOR } I = 1 \text{ TO } 11 \text{ STEP } 2$$

sets up a loop in which I will initially have the value 1, each time through the loop I will be increased by 2, and we will exit the loop when I is greater than 11. Another example is

$$100 \text{ FOR } I = 0 \text{ TO } 10$$

In this case I is initialized to 0, 1 is added to I each time through the loop, and we exit when I exceeds 10. In both examples, the statement NEXT I must be at the bottom of the loop and the number on the statement must be greater than 100.

BASIC, as is the case with most programming languages, has a library of functions associated with it. A programmer needs to read the documentation that comes with the BASIC system to find the names of these functions. A few that are common are SQR for square root, INT for converting a real quantity to an integer, and the trigonometric functions SIN, COS, TAN. These each take one argument. For example, if we wish to write a statement that calculates the square root of X and stores it in Y, we may write

$$100 \ Y = \text{SQR } (X).$$

A string is a sequence of characters. BASIC allows for string variables. This means that we may have variables whose values are strings. They are differentiated from numeric variables by using a $ in their names. For example, the variables X and $X\$$ indicate a numeric variable (X) and a string variable ($X\$$). BASIC contains the operations necessary for input, output, and comparison of strings.

A programmer may define a function as part of a BASIC program. The function may then be used in addition to the library functions. The user-defined functions may be numeric or string functions. This means that they may return to a numeric quantity or a string.

BASIC is useful for writing relatively short programs or programs for which execution speed is not of prime importance. However, if a BASIC compiler is available, then the execution speed may be increased. The user-friendliness of the language, the availability of the language, and its facilities for handling both numeric and character data make it an excellent language for beginners.

6.2 COBOL

COBOL is one of the most widely used programming languages for business applications. COBOL is an acronym for COmmon Business Oriented Language. The language was designed to be used in those situations that require decimal arithmetic and problems that require sophisticated use of files. It was also designed so that its statements are closer to English than to algebraic notation. Some say that COBOL is the most popular language because there are more lines of code written in COBOL than in any other language. Since it is generally a compiled language (translated to machine language before execution), programs written in COBOL execute faster than those run by an interpreter, such as BASIC.

A COBOL program is made up of four divisions: the identification division, the environment division, the data division, and the procedure division. The **identification division** is used as a place to put the program name, the author's name, the date written, and other remarks useful as documentation. The **environment division** is used to state any site- or machine-specific information, in order to make the program portable. All specifications of data, in complete detail, are made in the **data division**. The **procedure division** contains executable statements that control the flow of operations performed. Statements must be numbered. The information required in all the divisions and the detail necessary in the data division make COBOL programs rather lengthy.

There are a variety of COBOL statements, including several that may be used in the data division, to describe the type, representation, and structure of data. Expressions may be arithmetic, character, or logical. Input/output statements include information regarding control of associated devices. COBOL has statements for simple selection (IF-ELSE) and multiple selection (CASE and GO TO DEPENDING). Loops and subroutines are implemented in a variety of ways. Loops, as I/O statements, are often tied to the characteristics of devices associated with the computer.

COBOL allows for real, integer, character, and decimal data along with arithmetic operations usually needed in a business application. A collection of data structures are also available. These include tables (arrays) and records which may be specified by the programmer. Additionally, the language provides capabilities for extensive work with several types of files: sequential, direct-access, and indexed. The latter is particularly useful in a situation where rapid access to information is essential, such as in a database application.

COBOL is one of the most entrenched and frequently used programming languages in the commercial sector. It is criticized as verbose, but it provides the capabilities for writing programs which deal with large amounts of structured information in an efficient manner.

6.3 FORTRAN

FORTRAN was the first high-level programming language to come into widespread use. It was originated by a team of mathematicians and scientists working for IBM. FORTRAN is an acronym for FORmula TRANslator and has been used primarily for applications in the sciences, economics, and engineering. A great deal of scientific software currently exists in FORTRAN, primarily used on mainframes or minicomputers. Since it is generally a compiled language (translated to machine language before execution), programs written in FORTRAN execute faster than those run by an interpreter such as BASIC.

FORTRAN was designed in the mid-1950s and much of its syntax is due to the fact that programs were represented by a sequence of 80-column cards. Each statement must be on a separate line. A FORTRAN statement must be in columns 7-72 of a line. Any characters to the right of column 72 are ignored. A C in the first column indicates that the line is a comment, used only for documentation. If there is not a C in the first column, then columns 1-5 are used for statement labels, and a character in column 6 indicates that the line is a continuation of the previous line.

77

A FORTRAN program is a sequence of statements. Any declaration statements, which are nonexecutable, must come first. These include a PROGRAM statement, statements to declare the names and types of variables, constants, and functions, statements to initialize and declare constants (PARAMETER statements), and statements to initialize variables (DATA statements). These are followed by the executable statements. These include assignment statements, input/output statements, IF statements for conditional execution, DO statements used for iteration, GO TO statements used to transfer control from one portion of the program to another, statements used to call functions and subroutines, a STOP statement to terminate execution, and an END statement to mark the end of a program unit. Another type of statement is a FORMAT statement which allows precise control over the arrangement and contents of input and output.

Since FORTRAN is a "scientific" language, there is a full complement of mathematical functions available in the language. These are called the intrinsic functions. A programmer may write subprograms. These may be functions which take one or more arguments and return a single value of a simple data type, or subroutines which are used for more complex tasks or to modify an array. These functions and subroutines may be compiled separately from each other. This facilitates modular programming and software development.

There are six data types available in FORTRAN. They are INTEGER, REAL, DOUBLE PRECISION, COMPLEX, LOGICAL, and CHARACTER. The first four are arithmetic, and the operations available include

$$+,-, *,/, \text{ and } ** \text{ (exponentiation)}.$$

The operations

$$\text{.AND., .OR., and .NOT.}$$

are present for expressions that are type LOGICAL. Operations for objects of type CHARACTER include concatenation. The only data structures available are strings of characters and arrays.

FORTRAN is the oldest of the high-level languages in use today. Its use is widespread among the scientific and engineering communities. It lacks the control structures and data abstraction capabilities of more modern languages. Its longevity and the large amount of software written in FORTRAN for minicomputers and mainframe computers indicate that it will continue to be used in the future.

6.4 Pascal

Pascal was designed as a language to be used to teach programming. As such, it offers a wide range of control structures (if-then-else, case statements, for loops, while loops, repeat-until loops, etc.), has the ability to define data types both globally and locally, and allows for subprograms in the form of functions and procedures. These make the language rich enough to use in a variety of applications and to demonstrate simple and sophisticated programming concepts. It was developed by Niklaus Wirth and was first generally available in 1970.

A Pascal program is divided into several sections. Data structures available include one- and multidimensional arrays, sets, enumerated types, and pointers. Through the use of these and the TYPE block, a programmer may define, declare, and use other data structures. A programmer may define a function which takes one or more arguments and returns a value which is one of the simple data types of the language. Procedures may be used to return more complex objects such as arrays. Arguments may be passed to procedures or functions by value or by reference. Passing an argument by value means that only the value of the argument is available to the subprogram. Any changes to the argument are not communicated to the program that called the subprogram. Passing an argument by reference means that the address of the argument is available to the subprogram. In this case, the argument may be changed by the subprogram.

Pascal is a very good language for learning programming because it encourages and enforces the use of modern structured programming techniques. It is available on most systems and is appropriate for developing complex programs.

6.5　C Language

The programming language C is a high-level language with a rich collection of operators and data structures. It also includes several low-level features as well. This allows for bit-level manipulation of data. Designed and implemented in the early 1970s by Dennis Ritchie, it was originally to be used with the UNIX operating system. It has since become very popular and is widely available for use with various computer systems.

A C program consists of one or more functions. One function must be present whose name is **main**. All arguments are passed to functions by **value**. This means that a function cannot modify its arguments; it may return a single value associated with the name of the function. In order for a function to have an effect on more than one data item, the address of variables are often passed to functions. An effective programmer must therefore have a good grasp of the notion of a pointer. A pointer is a variable whose value is the address of another variable. While the correct use of pointers provides a powerful tool, a programmer must have a good understanding of the underlying machine.

All expressions in C have a value. Even assignment statements produce a value. If x has the value 5, then the statement

$$y = x + 1,$$

stores 6 in y and the statement has the value 6. C programmers often use this feature to write efficient and compact programs. C has some operators that are not present in other languages. Examples of these are the pre- and post-increment operators, ++. If x has the value 5, then ++x has the value 6 and changes x to have the value 6. Also, if x has the value 5, then x++ has the value 5 and x has the value 6.

C provides for the definition of types built from the native types of the language by use of the **typedef** statement. It also allows for the construction of complex data structures by the use of the **struct** facility. This allows for construction and manipulation of structures such as trees and linked lists.

C was written by a professional programmer for use by professional programmers. It is powerful and flexible, but it must be used with some care and discipline. Its features allow for the relatively easy construction of powerful and complex programs which may be difficult to debug. It provides a variety of control structures including a very general **for** statement. It allows for the manipulation of bits and bytes, as well as the more complex structures mentioned above. Also, the language has facilities for dealing with sequential files. C is almost always implemented as a compiled language, and most C compilers produce efficient and fast programs.

6.6 Object-Oriented Programming

Programs written in procedural programming languages are organized into callable subprograms such as procedures and functions. Unfortunately, the data worked on internally by a subprogram only "lives" while the subprogram is being executed. This ultimately results in the main program keeping track of the data that is outside the scope of the subprograms. Since the main program maintains much of the data, it is impossible to effectively test and debug programs in smaller, more manageable modules. Thus, much of the testing and debugging has to be done on the entire program, which can, in the case of a very large program, be a complicated, unacceptably difficult, and time consuming process.

In contrast to procedures and functions, an object's data is maintained as long as that object is needed. This allows the programmer to encapsulate all of the data and methods needed for a particular task into an object, a separate logical unit. Because an object has its own data and methods, once it has been thoroughly tested it can be thought of almost as a black box—as long as it works, the programmer does not have to worry about what is inside.

Since a program that is created by using object-oriented programming is required to maintain only a very small amount of data (the objects keep track of most of the data), it is possible to test and debug programs in separate modules. Thus, the strictly object-oriented approach sharply reduces the time spent debugging.

Object-oriented languages such as C++ and Java have additional advantages. A feature called "inheritance" allows the programmer to build a hierarchy of structures, with more and more complex objects being created as extensions of simpler ones. Another feature called "polymorphism," the flip side of inheritance, allows dissimilar objects to be utilized by their common attributes.

6.6.1 Classes: Object Templates

A class is a set of data (the class variables) and the methods needed to modify that data. A class definition has two parts:

1. the class declaration (class NewClass, below),

2. the class body: the variable declarations and method definitions.

For example:

```
class NewClass {
    . . .
    class body
    . . .
}
```

A class is a template for an object, although that object will not exist until a program statement creating an instance of that class is executed. The following is an example of code statements that will create an instance of the class NewClass:

```
NewClass NC;
NC = new NewClass;
```

The first statement above declares NC to be an object of the type NewClass. Then, the second statement allocates the memory space and creates the machine code necessary for an instance of the class NewClass to exist. Messages may now be sent to, and operations carried out by, the object NC.

The following is the definition of a simple class with one variable and no methods:

```
class Geometric {
    protected float area;
}
```

In the above example, area is declared as a protected variable of the type float (for floating point). A protected variable can only be accessed by methods of its own class, or by methods of a subclass of itself—in this case it would have to be the methods of a subclass, because Geometric has no methods. Most class variables are declared as protected or private (accessed only within its own class) so they can be encapsulated or "hidden." When class variables are encapsulated, the programmer does not have to be concerned about the class's internal data.

The following is the definition of a subclass of Geometric:

```
class Rectangle extends Geometric {
    public float height, width;
    public void computeArea (float h, float w) {
        area = h * w;
    }
}
```

The class Rectangle is an example of inheritance, which means that it inherits all of the variables and methods, not declared private, of its superclass. In this case, the only class "member" inherited from the superclass, Geometric, is the variable area. But notice that that area is modified within the Rectangle subclass. In this example, the variables' height and width and the method computeArea( ) are declared as public, so they can be accessed from outside the class. Also notice that the computeAreas( ) method has a return type of void (no return value) and two parameters declared as float: h and w.

Another subclass of Geometric could be defined as follows:

```
class Triangle extends Geometric {
    public float height, width;
    public void computeArea (float h, float w) {
        area = h * w * (1 / 2);
    }
}
```

The next example shows a method, assignArea( ), that utilizes polymorphism. The code that caused that method first creates instances of the Rectangle class and the Triangle class. Next, the Rectangle object, and then the Triangle object are passed as parameters to assignArea( ), which then assigns the appropriate values to the variable area.

```
void assignArea (Geometric geomObj) {
    float ht, wdth;
    ht = geomObj.height;
    wdth = geomObj.width;
    geomObj.ComputeArea (ht, wdth);
}
    . . .

Rectangle R;
R = new Rectangle;
R.height = 10.3;              // Assign height for rectangle
R.width = 3.4;               // Assign width for rectangle
assignArea (R);              // Assign area for rectangle
Triangle T;
T = new Triangle;
T.height = 4.17;             // Assign height for triangle
T.width = 9.2;1              // Assign width for triangle
assignArea (T);             // Assign area for triangle
    . . .
```

The above code is an example of polymorphism because when the Rectangle and Triangle objects were passed to the assignArea( ) method, they were both represented internally as the object geomObj, but the area was computed differently. In other words, the same message was passed to the same object, but the response was different.

In this section we will include Visual Basic, even though it is not considered a true object-oriented language (it does not allow multiple inheritance), because it does have objects. Also, C++ and Java are discussed in sections 6.6.3 and 6.6.4.

6.6.2 Visual Basic

Visual Basic is a result of the evolution of BASIC since its early days. The driving forces behind this continuing evolution have been:

1. much more powerful personal computers with the ability to process high resolution graphics,

2. a change in the perception of how a user should interact with a program, and

3. the incorporation of some of the better features of other languages.

Until about ten years ago, a user's interaction with software was limited. It involved the software guiding the user through the program step by step. Perhaps the program would ask a question with only two possible responses—yes or no—or perhaps the user was presented with a limited menu from which to choose. But the program always dictated what the user could do. Today's programs are event driven. The user may move a mouse cursor and then click on a menu bar, a tool bar, or an icon. The user may press either a hot key or an accelerator key to skip one or even several steps, or the user may elect to edit data in a cell. The user may even switch to another program entirely. In today's software environment, the user is in control with the program waiting for events and then responding.

Visual BASIC (VB), the most popular version of BASIC, reflects the trend toward event driven programming in a windowing environment. However, BASIC's roots, as an easy to learn, programmer friendly language, have not been lost.

The VB development environment consists of a menu bar at the top of the screen, a tool bar directly beneath the menu bar, a tool box on the left, and the project explorer window on the upper right, which displays a tree structure of the current project's files. On the right beneath the project explorer window is the properties window. The properties window will be discussed shortly.

The center of the screen—the majority of the screen—is used to design the program's graphical user interface (GUI). Controls—graphical components—are dragged by a mouse from the tool box on the left and laid out on a rectangular "form," to build the GUI the user will see at runtime. Controls include command buttons, text boxes, dialog boxes, option buttons, check boxes, labels, etc. At any time, the programmer may select a control with a mouse click, causing its properties to automatically appear in the properties window. The programmer may then edit the control's properties. The properties may vary from one control to another, but in general, they include screen location coordinates, height and width dimensions, background and foreground colors, captions or titles, visible/invisible status, etc.

The form provides the basic structure for a VB program. Forms are resizable and relocatable, but usually the form that appears first at runtime is full-screen size and usually it contains quite a few controls. When the user interacts with the form's controls (e.g., presses a command button), other smaller forms (windows) may appear which contain their own controls.

A form is a special type of control that may contain other controls. Since a form is a control, its properties can also be edited by the programmer during the design phase. For example, the screen location coordinates, the height and width dimensions, and the form's title are form properties.

All controls, including forms, are assigned names by the programmer making an entry in the name field of the properties window. VB automatically maintains a file for each form which has the same name as the form's property name. The programmer edits the form's code by going to the project explorer window and clicking on the form's file name. The view code window appears displaying the form's code. The code for a particular form consists of the event procedures for the various controls that are contained in the form. The event procedure for a mouse click on a command button named Calculate might be:

```
Sub cmdCalculate_Click ( )
        Call Calc ( ) Call     ' Call subroutine to calculate
    End Sub
```

Event procedures take the form: Sub abrControlName_Event where abr is the formal abbreviation for the control, ControlName is the control's name property, and Event is the formal event type. Some examples of control abbreviation are: cmd for command button, lbl for a label, and txt for a text box. Some examples of event types are Click for a mouse click, DblClick for a double mouse click, and KeyDown for a keypress. VB automatically calls the appropriate procedure for any control event on a particular form, unless the procedure does not exist, then it is ignored.

Some properties cannot be changed during runtime, for example the name property. But others can be. A good example is the programmer inserting code in an event procedure to change the visible/invisible property in order to make a dialog box appear.

A VB project also includes a standard module file for procedures and variables that are common to more than one form of module. Clicking the standard module file in the project explorer window causes the file to appear in the code view window, where it can be edited.

The Dim keyword, a holdover from the old BASIC, is used to declare variables. For example, Dim bytVal As Byte. Other variable types include:

1. Integer—16-bit integers,

2. Long—32-bit integers,

3. Single—32-bit floating point numbers,

4. Double—64-bit floating point numbers,

5. Currency—64-bit dollar amounts,

6. Boolean—Boolean variables, and

7. String—zero to 65,400 alphanumeric characters.

It is a VB convention to begin a variable name with a small letter and also with the first three letters the data type (e.g., Dim douTotal As Double).

VB also allows a variable to be declared as Variant. If a variable is not declared, it is assumed to be a Variant. VB performs automatic type conversions when a Variant variable is acted on by an arithmetic, assignment, comparison, or concatenation operator.

The ends of VB statements are indicated by carriage returns. A statement can be continued on the next line with the use of the underscore, "_", for example:

douDoubleVal = douDoubleVal1 + douDoubleVal2 + _
                       douDoubleVal3

The VB If statement has two forms:

If (Boolean expr.)   Then   statement(s)   End If
If (Boolean expr.)   Then   statement(s)
Else statement(s)   End If

The If Then Else statement is mutually exclusive. The Select Case statement is available if a decision requires additional branches.

VB has five control loops:

Do While   (Boolean expr.)   statement(s)   Loop
Do   statement(s)   Loop While   (Boolean expr.)
Do Until   (Boolean expr.)   statement(s)   Loop
Do   statement(s)   Loop Until   (Boolean expr.)
For Int = StartInt to EndInt   statement(s)   Next Int

The While keyword indicates loop while the Boolean expression is true. The Until keyword indicates loop until the Boolean expression is false. The For loop may also specify a step increment other than 1. If the step increment is negative, VB will count down to the ending integer value.

In addition to procedures defined using the Sub keyword shown earlier, VB allows the programmer to define functions using the Function keyword. Both types of procedures accept pass by value and pass by reference parameters, with only pass by reference parameters changed. Function declarations have the following form:

Function FunctionName (param. list) As ReturnType

Visual Basic is not a true object-oriented language because it does not allow inheritance. However, it does have objects. For example, controls are objects. Properties of controls are accessed during runtime using the same type of notation commonly used to access object members in other languages. For example, the caption property of a command button could be assigned in this way:

cmdButton.Caption = "Quit"

VB also provides system objects for Input/Output. An example is the Printer system object whose Print method can be accessed to send output to the printer as follows:

Printer.Printer Tab (0); "This is a print out message"

In addition, the programmer can define classes and create instances of classes with the New keyword.

Although a compiler is used to create executable files, VB provides an interpreter with extensive debugging features. With the interpreter, the program can be tested immediately, without waiting for the compiler to finish.

Advanced features include:

1. image controls that provide the capability of graphics images including animation,

2. programmer friendly Internet access (an application may actually bring the user out onto the Internet), and

3. the ability to add controls to the tool box, including Active-X controls which are found on Web sites.

6.6.3   C++

Except for the keywords and constructs that are concerned with object-oriented programming, C++ is almost identical to C language.

C++ classes are usually defined with only variable declarations and method prototypes. The methods are subsequently elaborated. It is traditional to place the class definitions in header files with the .h extension (eg. classdef.h), and to place the method implementation in a source code file with the .cc extension (source.cc).

Class definitions may have sections with the following accessibility:

1. public—accessible anywhere,

89

2. private—accessible from only the class itself, and

3. protected—accessible from the class and its subclasses.

Constructor methods are used to construct an object when the new keyword is used to create an instance of a class. Constructors have the same name as the class and no return type. They are so common, they are usually included in the class definition.

An example of a class definition is:

```
class Apartment {
    private:
        int nmbrOfUnits;
    public:
        Apartment (float perUnit, int apts) {
                rent = perUnit;
                nmbrUnits = apts;
        };
    protected:
        float getTotal ( );
        float rent;
};
```

The Apartment method is the constructor method. The implementation of the getTotal() method would be as follows:

```
float Apartment::getTotal ( ) {
        return (rent * nmbrUnits);
};
```

C++ allows for subclasses to inherit the methods and class variables of the "base" class. A subclass of Apartment might be:

```
class duplex : public Apartment {
    public:
        duplex (float perUnit, int apts = 2) {
                rent = perUnit;
        };
};
```

In addition to simple inheritance, C++ also allows for a class to be derived from more than one base class. This feature is known as multiple inheritance.

C++ provides a "preprocessor," which performs preliminary tasks for the compiler. The #include preprocessor directive can be used to include class definition files, for example:

#include mydef.h

The #include directive can also be used to include library classes. The #ifdef and #if directives are used for conditional compilation. The #define directive is used to define constants.

6.6.4 Java

Among computer languages, Java is most closely related to C/C++, upon which it was based. In fact, in many ways, Java is a slimmed down, simpler version of C++. For example, in Java there are no pointers, multiple inheritance, or operator overloading. Java also has automatic memory management capability, relieving the programmer of most of the responsibility of allocating and de-allocating blocks of memory.

Java, in an important sense, is a more direct way to program than C/C++ because it is not implementation or platform specific. An example of this is its floating-point numbers which, unlike other languages, are not designed for a specific CPU, but instead conform to the IEEE 754-1985 standard. Thus, the number of bits of a single-precision floating-point number is the same regardless of the system that is being programmed. In general, Java programs are completely portable. This is achieved by the Java compiler outputting a form of intermediate code called byte-code, with the byte-code later executed by an interpreter, which *is* system specific.

Another way that Java has made an attempt to be more universal than C/C++ and other earlier languages is by supporting the world-wide Unicode standard for coding of characters. Java characters can be selected from almost any alphabet, such as Arabic-Indic, for example, rather than just the Latin-alphabet supported by the ASCII standard.

In some important ways, Java has made a complete break from C/C++. It is an object-oriented programming language that completely severs the ties with procedural programming. There are no functions or procedures in Java. This simplifies the task of programmers and developers by allowing them to concentrate on the creation and programming of objects.

However, in other respects, there is more to learn in Java, because it has added advanced features. There are two types of Java programs: Applets, which require an Internet browser or an Applet viewer, and stand-alone applications. Java also has extensive library classes and built-in networking capability.

Java Name Space

Java was intended to support dynamic loading of modules, including loading of modules from anywhere on the Internet. For this reason, Java designers went to great lengths to avoid name space conflicts. There is no such thing as global variables or methods. All variables and methods are defined within a class or within an "interface" (interfaces are discussed shortly). There are two kinds of variables: class variables, called fields, and method variables, which are declared within a method and can not be accessed outside that method. The fields and methods of a class or interface are referred to as the members of that class or interface.

An interface defines the broad outline of how a class might be implemented and is Java's attempt to compensate for not allowing multiple inheritance—a class may implement more than one interface. An interface consists only of variables declared as static final (the Java equivalent of constants) and abstract methods (methods with a declaration part, but no method body). Any class that implements that interface must fully implement the body of all of the interface's abstract methods.

The first statement of a Java source file is the package statement. The following example of a package statement conveys that the classes and interfaces in that source file are part of a package, whose name is insurance, and that insurance is in turn a subpackage of another package, whose name is funds:

package funds.insurance;

The components of the package name must be the same as the components of the directory where the Java interpreter will find the package relative to the Java system directory. The directory where the interpreter would find the package of the above example would be:

/funds/insurance

Any class may be accessed within its own package and any class declared public may be accessed from outside its own package. However, even if the class is declared public, any class member declared private can not be accessed, except from within its own class. If a member of a public class is declared public, it can be accessed from other classes including from classes outside its own package. If a member of a public class is declared protected, it can still be accessed from a subclass of itself, even if the subclass is in a different package. Note: Unlike C++, Java declares members public, private, or protected individually, not in sections.

Class members are accessed using a hierarchical notation. Assume the package named insurance, from the above example, included a public class named Annuity, and that the class Annuity included a public method named calculateIncome. It could be accessed from any package in the following manner:

income = funds.insurance.Annuity.calculateIncome ( );

If a class is imported, members of that class may be accessed with abbreviated notation. For example:

import funds.insurance.Annuity;
income = Annuity.calculateIncome ( );

In most cases, import statements immediately follow the package statement, however, they can come anywhere.

As can be seen, Java has created a name space hierarchy that makes name space conflicts virtually impossible. A possible exception is if two classes with the same name are imported from different packages. In this case, the classes must be referenced by fully qualified notation rather than by abbreviated notation.

Java's developers have taken the concept of unique name identification a step further by proposing the inclusion of the Internet domain name, in reverse order, in package names used to access the Internet. For example, if a class were imported from an organization whose domain was mutual.com, the import statement might be:

import com.mutual.funds.insurance.Annuity

Some Important Differences Between Java and C/C++

Java has no preprocessor—it does not need one. There is no equivalent of the #include, #ifdef, #if, or #define directives.

The #include directive is not needed for two reasons:

1. Java does not make a distinction between declaring methods and method definitions, so there is no need to include header files, and

2. the use of fully qualified names for library classes means that the Java compiler knows exactly where to find them, so it does not need a special directive to tell it where to look.

The #ifdef and #if directives are used for conditional compilation, which Java does not need because it is platform independent.

Also, Java has no use for the equivalent of the #define directive, used to define constants, because it does not allow global names. The Java equivalent of a constant is a static final variable declared within a class of interface.

As mentioned earlier, internal character variable representation is based on the Unicode standard rather than the ASCII standard used in C/C++. This means that variables of type char in Java require sixteen bits versus the only eight bits required for C/C++. Boolean variables in Java are simpler to work with, having only two values— true and false. In C/C++, false is represented with a zero, with any other value considered to be true.

Unlike C/C++, character strings are not primitive data types, but instances of the class String. Java Strings are immutable objects which can not be appended. A programmer who wants to append a string must use another class, the StringBuffer class. However, both Java and C/C++ assign strings by enclosing the character string in double quotes.

Both Java and C++ use the new keyword to create an instance of an object. However, the C++ equivalent of the delete keyword and the free() method is not present in Java. Java instead relies on a technique called garbage collection, which runs in the background, to automatically free memory no longer in use.

Building a Graphical User Interface (GUI) in Java

Nearly all the controls described in the Visual Basic section are represented in the java.awt (Java Abstract Window Toolkit) library class. But in Java they are called components, rather than controls. A GUI is built by adding components to a special type of component called a container, which can contain other components. The most commonly used type of container is a frame, which is probably the closest Java equivalent to the Visual Basic form. Programming with the java.awt library class is, however, much more complex, with component classes and subclasses having numerous methods and class fields that must be understood.

For those interested in programmer friendliness, there is a form of Java called Visual Java available.